INDIANA'S PERFECT RUN to the **COLLEGE FOOTBALL NATIONAL CHAMPIONSHIP**

NEVER DAUNTED

RICH JANZARUK/HERALD-TIMES

99
8
7
2026

On fourth-and-4 from Miami's 12, Fernando Mendoza, on a designed draw, fights his way to a fourth-quarter touchdown and a 24-14 Indiana lead. GRACE HOLLARS/INDYSTAR

THE LINEUP

Sports editor
Nat Newell

Assistant sports editor
Aaron Ferguson

Executive editor
Ryan Martin

Beat reporters
Zach Osterman
Michael Niziolek

Columnist
Gregg Doyel

Photographers
Rich Janzaruk
Grace Hollars

Proofreader
Sherrill Amo

Project coordinator
Gene Myers

Special thanks
Alicia Del Gallo
Chris Thomas
Noah Amstadter
Josh Williams
Clarissa Young
Clarissa Shine
Jared Sábado-Hernández

Content packaged by Mojo Media, Inc.
Joe Funk
Jason Hinman

GRACE HOLLARS/INDYSTAR

ABOUT THE BOOK: *Never Daunted* condenses a year's worth of the world's best coverage of the Indiana Hoosiers from The Indianapolis Star and The Bloomington Herald-Times. For continuing coverage of the Hoosiers, go to indystar.com and heraldtimesonline.com. Order a print subscription or access the eNewspaper at subscribe.indystar.com/offers and subscribe. heraldtimesonline.com/offers. This book includes coverage from the USA TODAY Network, which includes IndyStar and The Herald-Times.

USA TODAY SPORTS
The Herald-Times
IndyStar. PART OF THE USA TODAY NETWORK

Front cover photo by RICH JANZARUK/HERALD-TIMES
Back cover photo by GRACE HOLLARS/INDYSTAR

PRINTED IN U.S.A.
ISBN: 979-8-89855-004-2

This is an unofficial publication. This book is in no way affiliated with, licensed by or endorsed by the NCAA or Indiana University.

TRIUMPH BOOKS
TRIUMPHBOOKS.COM
@TRIUMPHBOOKS

814 North Franklin Street
Chicago, Illinois 60610
Phone: (312) 337-0747

The Herald-Times | IndyStar. PART OF THE USA TODAY NETWORK

NEVER DAUNTED

INDIANA'S PERFECT RUN to the COLLEGE FOOTBALL NATIONAL CHAMPIONSHIP

1

THE CHAMPS

To beat Miami for the national championship, Fernando Mendoza delivered the biggest play in IU history.

16

THE SEASON

Without down-the-stretch heroics at Iowa, Oregon and Penn State, 2025 would have been a disappointment.

84

THE B1G TITLE

Gritty victory over Ohio State produces Indiana's first outright conference crown since 1945.

94

THE HEISMAN

By winning the 91st Heisman Trophy, Mendoza does what no Hoosier had done before.

102

THE GLORY

Down go Alabama, Oregon and Miami in the CFP as Hoosiers march to their first championship.

INTRODUCTION

THE GREATEST COLLEGE FOOTBALL STORY EVER TOLD

BY ZACH OSTERMAN | JANUARY 19, 2026

Curt Cignetti arrived in Bloomington in 2023 with self-confidence somehow stronger than the historic, frustrating culture of defeat hardened into Indiana's football program.

In two short years, that steadfast belief in his ability, his process and his people turned the Hoosiers into the dominant force in the sport, their newfound power delivering an unlikely yet undisputable first national championship in program history.

Across the course of 2025 — and into 2026 — IU football flattened a path over everything and everyone in front of it.

Cignetti's team dismantled Illinois, swept its rivalry series with Michigan State and Purdue, twice defeated Oregon, punched past Ohio State in the Big Ten title game and rudely dismissed Alabama in the Rose Bowl.

Along the way, the Hoosiers realized other program firsts, including a perfect regular season, record-setting television audiences in the conference championship game and the Rose Bowl, and, of course, Fernando Mendoza's Heisman Trophy triumph.

This performance rearranged all we thought was possible for Indiana football and upended so many of college football's fundamental conventions.

This was not supposed to be possible. Not in America's ultimate cement-ceiling sport. Nowhere else in our shared experience is your past supposed to define your present and inform your future.

In this way, the Hoosiers became revolutionaries, making better use than anyone else in America of ideas once considered radical — the transfer portal, immediate eligibility, player compensation — to turn a perennial cellar dweller into the most ruthless, terrifying team in the country.

At the heart of it all was this brash, assured western Pennsylvanian, the son of a hall-of-famer who got his own start in head coaching late and, no matter where he went, wasted zero effort making up for the time he'd lost.

From the moment he arrived in Indiana, Cignetti remained steadfast in one of his fundamental beliefs: There would be no self-imposed limitations in Bloomington anymore. With a speed no one could have expected, Cignetti turned words into wins.

All of it culminated in Miami Gardens, against Miami (Florida), Indiana plowing past the Hurricanes and using Hard Rock Stadium as a coronation site for the kind of immortality fans of this program probably wouldn't have even allowed themselves to dream about.

The Hoosiers' achievement now sets in stone for all time. Impossible made into forever. The greatest college football story ever told.

Indiana football, a national champion. ■

IndyStar has crafted several commemorative page prints celebrating milestone moments during Indiana's championship run. Clockwise from the left: IU's first outright Big Ten title since 1945, Fernando Mendoza becoming the first Hoosier to win the Heisman Trophy, the front page distributed at the stadium after the national championship game, and a page celebrating the win over Miami and IU's first football natty. These page prints and several others are available for purchase starting at $27. Go to usatodaystore.com and search Indiana.

2021 PULITZER PRIZE WINNER

THE INDIANAPOLIS STAR

SATURDAY, DECEMBER 6, 2025
"Where the Spirit of the Lord is, there is liberty" II COR. 3:17

IndyStar.

PART OF THE USA TODAY NETWORK

2025 BIG TEN CHAMPIONSHIP COMMEMORATIVE EDITION

13 NO. 2 INDIANA VS. NO. 1 OHIO STATE LUCAS OIL STADIUM, INDIANAPOLIS 10

UNDISPUTED!

13-0 HOOSIERS CAPTURE FIRST CONFERENCE TITLE SINCE 1967

Indiana quarterback Fernando Mendoza celebrates with the Grange-Griffin Trophy as the most valuable player of the Big Ten championship game. With a 13-10 victory, the Hoosiers (13-0) beat top-ranked Ohio State (12-1) for the first time since 1988, won their first Big Ten title since 1967 and earned their first outright conference title since 1945. GRACE HOLLARS/INDYSTAR

THE INDIANAPOLIS STAR

SATURDAY, DECEMBER 13, 2025
"Where the Spirit of the Lord is, there is liberty" II COR. 3:17

IndyStar.

PART OF THE USA TODAY NETWORK

2025 HEISMAN TROPHY COMMEMORATIVE EDITION

JAZZ AT LINCOLN CENTER, NEW YORK CITY

HeisMendoza!

INDIANA'S QUARTERBACK CAPTURES COLLEGE FOOTBALL'S HIGHEST HONOR

Indiana quarterback Fernando Mendoza broke down after winning the Heisman Trophy — the first Hoosier to win college football's top prize. Then he delivered a heartwarming speech, at times in Spanish. He dominated the voting over runner-up Diego Pavia of Vanderbilt: 643 to 189 in first-place votes and 2,362 to 1,435 in total points. Mendoza passed for 2,980 yards with 33 touchdowns and rushed for 240 yards with six touchdowns. BRAD PENNER/IMAGN IMAGES

HOW THEY VOTED FOR THE 91ST HEISMAN TROPHY

FERNANDO MENDOZA	DIEGO PAVIA	JEREMIYAH LOVE	JULIAN SAYIN	JACOB RODRIGUEZ
Indiana	Vanderbilt	Notre Dame	Ohio State	Texas Tech
Quarterback	Quarterback	Running back	Quarterback	Linebacker
2,362 points	1,435 points	719 points	432 points	295 points

2021 PULITZER PRIZE WINNER

THE INDIANAPOLIS STAR

MONDAY, JANUARY 19, 2026
"Where the Spirit of the Lord is, there is liberty" II COR. 3:17

IndyStar.

PART OF THE USA TODAY NETWORK

27 21

COLLEGE FOOTBALL PLAYOFF NATIONAL CHAMPIONSHIP
HARD ROCK STADIUM, MIAMI GARDENS, FLORIDA

16-0!

HOOSIERS COMPLETE THE GREATEST COLLEGE FOOTBALL STORY EVER

2021 PULITZER PRIZE WINNER

THE INDIANAPOLIS STAR

MONDAY, JANUARY 19, 2026
"Where the Spirit of the Lord is, there is liberty" II COR. 3:17

IndyStar.

PART OF THE USA TODAY NETWORK

CHAMPS!

HOOSIERS COMPLETE PERFECT SEASON WITH FIRST NATIONAL CHAMPIONSHIP

THE CHAMPS

GRACE HOLLARS/INDYSTAR

FROM IMPROBABLE TO UNSTOPPABLE

WHEN MENDOZA ROSE TO THE OCCASION AGAIN, INDIANA OWNED ITS FIRST NATIONAL CHAMPIONSHIP

BY GREGG DOYEL | JANUARY 19, 2026

The confetti flying around Hard Rock Stadium is crimson and cream, and so is the 2025 college football national champion as the pro-Indiana crowd celebrates the Hoosiers' 27-21 victory over Miami (Florida) in the College Football Playoff championship game by serenading Fernando Mendoza — while the IU quarterback dissolves into tears.

The emotions were real Monday night at Miami Gardens, Florida, and so was the result, and if you're pinching yourself just understand something: You are not alone.

Indiana football, the losingest program in college football history entering the season, now presides over everyone, everywhere, after running roughshod through a 16-game schedule capped by a Big Ten championship game victory over No. 1 Ohio State, routs in the Rose Bowl over No. 9 Alabama and in the Peach Bowl over No. 5 Oregon, and now this wire-to-wire victory over No. 10 Miami.

And when it was over, and the individual awards had been handed out —Mendoza as offensive player of the game; quarterback-chasing, punt-blocking Mikail Kamara as defensive player of the game — the man everyone wanted to hear speak was given the microphone.

And you know IU coach Curt Cignetti: He did not disappoint.

"Best fans in America!" Cignetti shouted at an IU football fan base that was almost as revelatory as the team it supported, having filled up most of the Rose Bowl and all of the Peach Bowl and even here — at the Miami Hurricanes' home stadium, no less — taking over at least 60% of Hard Rock Stadium.

As the fans were roaring, all of them still here — if you'd come all the way to Miami, would you have missed *this* moment? — Cignetti led the crowd in one last cheer.

"I know what you want!" Cignetti bellowed. "Did you ever think this was possible? On three: One, two, three ... Hoo, hoo, hoo — HOOSIERS!"

MENDOZA'S TD RUN FOR THE AGES

Fernando Mendoza wasn't all that good until he had to be. And then he was great — Heisman great, No. 1 NFL draft pick great, national champion great.

And his greatness in the final minutes started as so many things do around this IU football team: with sharp words from Cignetti.

What did the IU coach say to his quarterback with 11:28 left in the game and the Hoosiers clinging to a 17-14 lead and facing fourth-and-5 at the Miami 37? That will stay between coach and quarterback, but this is how it looked:

Cignetti walking circles around the IU players circled on the field, pacing, letting his assistant coaches handle the specifics — delegating, as he does — until he could bite his tongue no longer. Cignetti stalks up to Mendoza, who

Fernando Mendoza celebrates after his incredible 12-yard rushing touchdown gave Indiana a 10-point fourth-quarter lead. The quarterback draw on fourth down was the signature play of the College Football Playoff. GRACE HOLLARS/INDYSTAR

2026
INDIANA
15

to that point is 13 of 23 passing for 134 yards, with three sacks and minus-20 yards rushing.

Mendoza has taken a beating all game, not all of it legal, as Miami has hit him late and hit him in the head — and sometimes hit him late *by* hitting him in the head. But the time for Cignetti to commiserate with Mendoza over his toughness, his poise, will come later. Right now, he's getting nose-to-nose with his quarterback, challenging him, spitting out a handful of words and driving home his point by jabbing his finger before stomping off.

Mendoza doesn't blink. Seconds later he's dropping back — it's fourth-and-5, remember — and hitting Charlie Becker with a back-shoulder pass of 19 yards. That was a Heisman throw, but he's about to unleash a mythical run, a play that will join Omar Cooper Jr.'s leaping, toe-tapping TD catch against Penn State as the most memorable moments in IU football history.

It's fourth down again — fourth-and-4 at the Miami 12 — and Cignetti sends out his field-goal team. But then he gets to thinking, and he doesn't like it at all, and he's calling a time-out to send the offense back out. The call is a quarterback draw, and the play is designed to go left, but when Mendoza reaches the line of scrimmage, he spots a seam to the right and cuts that way. Mendoza runs like a newborn colt, thin legs wobbling all over the place, but he's running into two Miami defenders at the 5-yard line, bouncing off both, spinning 360 degrees and spotting the end zone.

Mendoza has the first down, but he wants more. He's diving for the end zone, stretching the ball across the goal line as he's being speared in the ribs, but he hangs onto the ball and the Hoosiers lead 24-14.

"He ran a linebacker over," Cignetti said. "His will — he wasn't going to be denied."

That touchdown gave the Hoosiers a 24-14 lead with 9:18 left, just enough to withstand the Hurricanes' final rally.

"On the first fourth down," Mendoza said, "Charlie Becker made a fantastic catch. On the second fourth down, I would die for my guys."

CIGNETTI TAKES IU FROM WORST TO FIRST

Remember *Indinia?* That was just four seasons ago, the 2021 opener against Iowa. IU freshman running back David Holloman — no fault of his — wore a jersey with "Indinia" printed on the back. The image went viral. That was the only way IU football could go viral, four seasons ago.

Remember 2-10? That was the Hoosiers' record that season. They beat Idaho and Western Kentucky. Lost to everyone else, including all nine Big Ten opponents. Pick a low moment: The 54-7 loss to Ohio State? How about 38-3 against Rutgers? No — 44-7 against Purdue.

Things were bleak in 2021, and they stayed bleak in '22 (4-8) and '23 (3-9).

Then IU hired Curt Cignetti.

The rest of the story is kind of like what Cignetti was yelling to the crowd after Monday's game:

Did you ever think this was possible?

Of course not. Not the trip to the 2024 CFP playoffs in his first year, not the No. 1 national ranking this season, not those eye-popping scores, one more improbable than the last. IU beat Oregon 56-22 and Alabama 38-3 in the CFP bracket, but does anyone remember the score of the Illinois game in September? The Illini were ranked No. 8 in the country.

Indiana won 63-10.

It reads like a misprint, every single fact about the rise of IU football, but as Cignetti was saying as the CFP title game approached, the time for fairy tales was over.

"I think it's time to sharpen the saw now, throw those warm fuzzies out the door, that sentimentalism," Cignetti said. "We've got to have a sharp edge going into this game. You don't go to war with warm milk and cookies."

A CHAMPIONSHIP? EMOTIONS POUR OUT

The saw was sharp early. IU was bludgeoning Miami, beating the blue-collar, ground-and-pound Hurricanes at their game. IU running backs Kaelon Black and Roman Hemby were on the way to combining for 139 yards on 36 car-

Miami's imposing defensive line lived up to the hype, but running back Kaelon Black still carried the ball 17 times for a gritty 79 yards. GRACE HOLLARS/INDYSTAR

74
B1G
INDIANA
2026
8

ries while the IU defense was bottling up the Miami offense.

Miami got rolling in the second half, big plays from running back Mark Fletcher Jr. and quarterback Carson Beck and electric receiver Malachi Toney — and for a while there, Indiana's saw was losing its serrated edge. Mendoza was sacked repeatedly. The defense was punctured for big plays. Miami was coming back.

And then Mikail Kamara blocked a punt. It wasn't even a designed punt-block play. In fact, it was a "punt safe" play — designed to get a big return. But Kamara felt he had come close to blocking the previous punt, and as Miami prepared to punt on fourth-and-1 at its 16, Kamara said he decided "to shoot my shot." He raced around one Miami player, then another, reaching out with his right hand to block the punt into the end zone. Teammate Isaiah Jones recovered it for a 17-7 lead.

Indiana was back in control, and with Mendoza making Heisman plays — legacy plays — in the fourth quarter, the Hoosiers were one defensive stand from finishing off the impossible story. And here it came, an interception by cornerback Jamari Sharpe with 44 seconds left.

Pretty soon the confetti was firing from every corner of the stadium, and fans were running onto the field and making snow angels in the shredded pieces of crimson-and-cream. Cignetti was thinking about his dad, Frank Sr., who died in 2022 at age 84, pointing toward heaven as he walked onto the field after the final horn.

Later, in the postgame news conference, Kamara and Cignetti talked about what IU had just done.

"I didn't think it was possible, man — I can't lie," Kamara said.

Said Cignetti: "We're 16-0. We're national champions at Indiana University, which I know a lot of people thought wasn't possible. It's probably one of the greatest sports stories of all time."

Out on the field, where Mendoza was talking to ESPN's Holly Rowe, he was calling this "the most special moment of my life" before bursting into tears. At that moment, whoever runs the Hard Rock Stadium public address system got silly, playing the 1976 song "Fernando" by ABBA. More than 40,000 IU fans, still hanging around, sang along. They had waited decades for this moment, through all those losses and moments like "Indinia" and scores like Rutgers 38, Indiana 3.

Of course they waited, and now they were thanking their quarterback, and his teammates, for the perfect payoff.

"If I had to do it all again, I would my friend, Fernando ..." ■

Above: Wide receiver Elijah Sarratt has his celebratory moment with the championship trophy during the postgame festivities. GRACE HOLLARS/INDYSTAR

Opposite: Linebackers Isaiah Jones (46) and Rolijah Hardy (21) were flying high in the aftermath of teammate Mikail Kamara blocking a Miami punt, which was recovered in the end zone for a touchdown by Jones. GRACE HOLLARS/INDYSTAR

46
21

THE SEASON

JULIA HANSEN/IOWA CITY PRESS-CITIZEN

INDIANA
C. SMITH
65
96

THE NEXT STEP IS THE HARDEST

HOW DOES CIGNETTI CLOSE THE GAP WITH THE SPORT'S POWERHOUSES?

BY ZACH OSTERMAN | DECEMBER 22, 2024

Moments after Kurtis Rourke's first-quarter interception, Indiana defensive coordinator Bryant Haines was on the green dot to his captain. In all but name, linebacker Aiden Fisher served in that capacity for Haines' defense. Fisher played the same position Haines did during his career, and the one Haines coached in addition to coordinator duties. The two were so aligned, Haines said earlier in the 2024 season, they could finish each other's thoughts.

At that moment, with Notre Dame backed up inside its 5-yard line, Haines asked Fisher whether he wanted to dial up something aggressive, maybe play for a safety. No, Fisher said. Keep it conservative, trust the scheme. Seconds later, Jeremiyah Love pounced on a missed gap assignment and bounced outside, hitting the sideline for a 98-yard touchdown run.

As much as any one sequence could, those back-to-back plays changed Indiana's first College Football Playoff game for good. And in so doing, they delivered to Indiana a valuable lesson to take forward from its breakthrough season: At the summit of the sport, the small margins were everything.

"You misfit it a little bit and the thing rips you for 98 yards and six points," Haines said. "That's how small the margin for error is against elite teams. I felt that way against Ohio State. I felt that way again tonight."

Fair or not, those would be the two games against which Indiana's 11-2 season was judged nationally. It was a curse and a compliment.

For some, the Hoosiers' largely quiet 27-17 exit from the first round of the CFP — after reaching the field thanks in part to an undeniably forgiving schedule — was proof they never belonged in the first place. That this spot would have been better off in the hands of a three-loss SEC team or two-loss Miami (Florida).

Setting that argument to one side, the compliment was in what the argument itself said: IU football earned the right to be talked about among the most serious programs in the sport in 2024. They only yelled at you when you mattered.

There would be an understandable temptation to say Indiana got a long look, in the games that really tested the Hoosiers this season, at where they needed to improve. The opponents that beat Curt Cignetti's team — and let's make no mistake, beat it soundly — were bigger, stronger, faster, better.

In the most simplistic terms, that was true. Cignetti and staff had seven recruits visiting campus over the weekend before the holiday dead period hit, with needs at quarterback, along the defensive line and elsewhere. The Jimmys and the Joes remained the greatest priority.

"Everything is about recruitment and development," Cignetti said, "and now retention. Every year you've got to start over now in college football."

But for all the national handwringing about Indiana's performance in these games, the Hoosiers knew it was on small margins they turned. If anything, that made them even more painful to process.

IU struggled badly with crowd noise and pressure at Ohio State. And yet it was 7-7 and headed for a halftime tie before James Evans dropped the punt that served up the Buckeyes' go-ahead touchdown. And it was a rare special

Senior Zach Horton, an honorable mention All-Big Ten tight end after three years at James Madison, wept when Indiana's amazing season ended with a 27-17 loss to Notre Dame in the first round of the College Football Playoff. CHRISTINE TANNOUS/INDYSTAR

teams miscommunication — ball went one way, coverage team the other — that swung open the door for Caleb Downs' touchdown return.

Indiana lost that game by 25 and deserved to. But the moments that turned a challenging task into an impossible one were self-inflicted and imminently correctable mistakes.

As it was on this Friday night in South Bend.

The Hoosiers opened three-and-out, then on Riley Leonard's first pass of the game, James Carpenter pawed the ball into the air and D'Angelo Ponds picked it off. A holding penalty pushed IU back into minus territory before Rourke tore off a textbook 28-yard back-shoulder throw to Elijah Sarratt, the kind both players made routine during the season.

From shotgun, on first-and-10 at the Notre Dame 17, arguably the best red-zone quarterback in the country lined up behind center. Rourke had thrown 19 touchdowns from the 20 on in coming into this game. He finished the year completing better than 70% of his passes in the most compressed area of the field. He was a primary reason why Indiana was among the best red-zone teams in the country, if not the best.

And he promptly threw his first and only red-zone interception of 2024. On the next play, Haines toyed with getting aggressive, Fisher suggested taking a beat, IU misplayed the run and Jeremiyah Love was gone.

"I'll take the fall for that one," Fisher said. "We have to play our gaps better and play more disciplined."

It would be a vast oversimplification to say if Indiana had scored a touchdown on that possession, Love never scores and the Hoosiers win. It would not at all be an oversimplification to say that twice in a month, Indiana played the kinds of teams it would need to beat to entrench itself at this end of the sport. It lost games that turned against the Hoosiers not on glaring talent discrepancies but on the small things.

The indiscernible-to-the-naked-eye things. The only-see-it-later-on-film things. The stuff that stayed with you long after the fact, because it was easier to accept simply being outclassed than it was to spend an offseason wishing you could have had one moment back.

None of this was meant to damn a remarkable, historic season to second-class status.

Nobody in college football had more fun than Indiana fans in the fall of 2024, which was, it's worth remembering sometimes, the basic point of the enterprise.

And a team that refused to accept anyone's limitations — including its own — on what IU football was capable of realized success the Hoosiers had never previously known.

"I was in those locker rooms. I was at Indiana," said Haines, who spent a year as a graduate assistant under Kevin Wilson early in his career. "I know what it meant to be an Indiana football player in 2012, and these guys changed it forever."

Sixth-year center Mike Katic, who had seen this program rise and fall and rise again, said simply: "We changed the trajectory of Indiana football. We changed the way people think about Indiana football."

Wrapping into words all IU accomplished would ask for another 5,000, and that still wouldn't be enough. It should be hard to eulogize about something that never happened before.

Make no mistake, though, Cignetti was not. He estimated that Indiana's traveling party would arrive back in Bloomington a little before 4 a.m. Saturday, with a weekend full of visits on the schedule and a roster to restock.

College football didn't stop, and it wasn't forgiving. The Hoosiers entered 2025 with a target on their back and pressure on their performance. If they wanted back in the CFP, they would need to be even better.

So, they would need to carry with them the truest lesson of championship performance, in any sport: The closer you get to the top, the harder the climb, and the more perilous your steps. The finest margins could make you — or break you. ■

While the season ended in disappointment for Curt Cignetti and the Hoosiers, their 11-2 campaign served as a springboard to bigger and better things in 2025. CHRISTINE TANNOUS/INDYSTAR

'INDIANA WAS THE BEST PLACE'

HOW THE HOOSIERS LANDED ONE OF THE TRANSFER PORTAL'S TOP QBS

BY ZACH OSTERMAN | JANUARY 3, 2025

Fernando Mendoza entered the transfer portal eyes wide open, not just to the opportunities potential new teams presented, but to the ways he would be pushed to improve by their coaches.

A third-year sophomore, Mendoza passed for more than 3,000 yards in 2024, in his first full season as California's No. 1 quarterback. After starting the final eight games as a redshirt freshman, Mendoza showed across-the-board improvement as full-time starter. But, with his sights on the NFL as a long-term goal, Mendoza knew he needed to find a coaching staff and an offense that would push him to be even better.

Through conversations with and interest from a host of programs, including Georgia, Miami (Florida) and Missouri, the quarterback ranked No. 3 at his position in this offseason's portal cycle found what he was looking for in Bloomington. Other top signal callers in the portal were Georgia's Carson Beck (who landed with Miami) and Washington State's John Mateer (who landed with Oklahoma).

Mendoza's commitment to Indiana was first reported on Christmas Eve.

"I still believe I have a ton of things to get better at," Mendoza told IndyStar on Jan. 3, 2025. "Indiana was the best place for me to make that jump developmentally."

Across 21 games in Berkeley (20 of them starts), Mendoza passed for 4,712 yards and 30 touchdowns. Mendoza, born in Boston but raised in Miami, completed 66.5% of his passes leading the Bears to back-to-back bowls, and Mendoza cut his interception rate from one every 24.3 attempts to one every 64.3 attempts last season.

Three times last fall, Mendoza was selected ACC quarterback of the week.

Indiana jumped into his recruitment as soon as it could.

"The journey is a whirlwind," Mendoza said. "It happens so fast. My family and I had decided my time at Berkeley had come to an end. It was an amazing chapter in my life. After I entered my name into the portal, a couple very important schools reached out and had great conversations. I tried to get as much information as possible on every school."

The Hoosiers offered obvious appeal.

Dating to their time at James Madison, coach Curt Cignetti and offensive coordinator Mike Shanahan enjoyed substantial success fitting their scheme around transfer quarterbacks. Jordan McCloud won Sun Belt player of the year in his season working in their offense, in 2023, and Kurtis Rourke made second-team All-Big Ten while setting numerous single-season IU passing records last season.

But Indiana also enjoyed an added bonus — the personal experience of Mendoza's younger brother, Alberto, who redshirted his freshman season in Bloomington in 2024.

"I think having my little brother there, who's my best friend and the person who pushes me the hardest, it was great to have that, to see his perspective on the coaching staff, the culture," Fernando Mendoza said.

Mendoza visited Bloomington not long after entering the portal, where he spent time with several returning players. Cignetti's offense projects to return its top two leading receivers, Elijah Sarratt and Omar Cooper Jr., and IU added significant depth at running back via the portal.

All of which contributed to Mendoza's decision to commit to Indiana just before Christmas and sign on Dec. 30. He joined a quarterback room that looked and felt quite different than the one that steered IU through its historic 2024 season.

Rourke was headed for the NFL. His backup, Tayven Jackson, entered the portal after the season and landed at Central Florida.

Quarterback Fernando Mendoza played well in his two seasons as the starter at Cal, but Curt Cignetti and his staff had greater things in mind when they recruited him to Bloomington out of the transfer portal. PAUL KARGE/SHREVEPORT TIMES

Tyler Cherry, a four-star prospect in the 2024 class who flipped to IU from Duke after coaching changes, redshirted alongside the younger Mendoza. Cherry suffered a noncontact knee injury during CFP preparations and was questionable for fall camp. And the Hoosiers added a high school QB, Jacob Bell of Naperville, Illinois, who flipped from Ball State to IU on Christmas Day.

Position coach Tino Sunseri left after the loss to Notre Dame for UCLA, to coach quarterbacks and call plays for the Bruins. Cignetti tapped Chandler Whitmer, passing game specialist with the Atlanta Falcons, as Sunseri's replacement.

Between time as a graduate assistant at the college level and four years in numerous roles in the NFL, Whitmer worked alongside several successful quarterbacks, including Justin Fields, Trevor Lawrence, Justin Herbert, Kirk Cousins and Michael Penix. During his recruitment, Mendoza got the chance to talk with Whitmer, further reinforcing Indiana's appeal.

Ultimately, all those considerations — his brother's endorsement, Indiana's returning talent, the staff's track record of developmental and competitive success, and the opportunity in front of him — led Mendoza to Bloomington.

He joined a program Cignetti called "the emerging superpower of college football," Mendoza's dreams aligning with those of a program not content to rest on past success. All of it, Mendoza believed, was within reach.

"That was a huge thing for me," he said, "especially having seen their offense have success and having coach Shanahan and coach Cignetti being a part of really being able to grow their team, whether it's at Elon, JMU or Indiana. All those teams were successful and had really good quarterback play. I just thought, 'This is a great situation.'"

In mid-January, Cignetti listed Mendoza's attributes on the "ESPN College Football" podcast, including "he can throw the ball ... he can spin the ball ... he can make all the throws."

"He's pretty mobile," Cignetti said. "He throws well on the move. He can run. He runs better than Kurtis. He's a highly intelligent guy. That's where it all begins as everybody knows.

"We think he's going to give us something." ■

'YOUR ANTENNA IS ALWAYS UP'

HOW CIGNETTI KEPT INDIANA'S ROSTER AND COACHING STAFF INTACT

BY MICHAEL NIZIOLEK | AUGUST 24, 2025

Curt Cignetti knows better than most that success creates opportunity.

Cignetti climbed the coaching ranks from Division II all the way to the Power Four one winning season at a time.

He already has planted his flag in Bloomington — he signed a lucrative new extension after Indiana's 10-0 start in 2024 that will pay him $8 million a year through 2032 — but he recognized the Hoosiers' first appearance in the College Football Playoff would open doors for many of his coaches and players.

"Your antenna is always up," Cignetti told The Herald-Times in an offseason sit-down interview.

Cignetti managed to keep all eight players who won All-Big Ten honors, including three All-Americans, with eligibility left. He also was able to bring back all but one (quarterbacks coach Tino Sunseri) of his 10 on-the-field coaches.

Indiana was one of just five teams in the 18-team Big Ten that didn't change at least one of its coordinators. There were three teams in the conference — Maryland, Nebraska and Ohio State — that replaced offensive and defensive coordinators. And Cignetti had five coaches on his staff who had been with him for three or more seasons.

That continuity across the roster and coaching staff helped explain the confidence Cignetti had going into the 2025 season.

"I get questions, how are you going to sustain it?" Cignetti said at Big Ten media days. "We're not looking to sustain it. We're looking to improve it. And the way you do that is by having the right people on the bus, upstairs in the coaches' offices, downstairs in the locker room."

'ANXIOUS MOMENTS' OVERCOME TO KEEP TALENTED ROSTER INTACT

Indiana's draft hopefuls with eligibility left didn't keep fans waiting in the aftermath of a disappointing 27-17 opening-round CFP loss to Notre Dame.

Linebacker Aiden Fisher got the ball rolling by announcing plans to run it back for 2025 with a social media post two days after the game. Defensive end Mikail Kamara and cornerback D'Angelo Ponds quickly followed suit.

Wide receiver Elijah Sarratt said Cignetti gave players the space to make their decisions. They huddled with their families, but the general sentiment among the group was that if everyone came back, they would have the makings of another postseason contender.

There weren't any meaningful departures in the transfer portal, either.

The 13 scholarship players who entered the portal in the winter combined for 14 starts last season; cornerback Jamier Johnson accounting for 10 of those. The Hoosiers signed multiple experienced players at the position (Pitt's Ryland Gandy and Northern Illinois' Amariyun Knighten) before Johnson's departure even became official.

"They like the program, they believe in the program and they have relationships with each other and relationships with the coaches and (head strength coach) Derek (Owings)," Cignetti said. "They came into JMU and they developed and got a little chip on their shoulder, had something to prove and continued to develop. Why would you go somewhere else?"

Beyond the loyalty IU players felt toward Cignetti, he had the NIL resources at his disposal to keep everyone happy while remaining active in the portal.

Coach Curt Cignetti catches up on things with Indiana's president, Pam Whitten, in April 2025 before the start of the men's Little 500 bicycle race at Bill Armstrong Stadium. RICH JANZARUK/HERALD-TIMES

"I had a pretty good idea what my number would be early on, and so we were able to go to work," Cignetti said without revealing specific figures.

It was all smooth sailing until outside forces threatened to upend IU's feel-good offseason midway through spring camp. Cignetti, like many coaches, heard the whispers of big-money deals being offered to basketball players in the transfer portal ahead of an expected settlement in the House v. NCAA case.

There was initial optimism that the judge in the case would accept the terms of the settlement before the spring window for football opened for 10 days on April 16, but outstanding issues delayed final approval of the deal until June.

"That was the only time where there were some anxious moments," Cignetti said. "We had a couple kids come in and indicate that school X had reached out with big numbers. When spring ended, as the head coach, you were wondering who else might be coming to see you. We all read what was going on."

Cignetti told reporters at Big Ten media days that an unnamed team offered one of his players $1.5 million to enter the spring portal. He said in May that he had conversations with multiple players who received interest from other programs.

It made for a unique balancing act for Cignetti, who handled his team's purse strings. He wasn't one of the many collegiate coaches rushing to hire a general manager – "I'm the GM and the head coach" — and he had gone on record saying the process wasn't all that complicated.

The uncertainty in the spring was different — Cignetti had to proceed with caution as he looked to address a few needs coming out of camp while holding back enough funds to play a little defense.

"We really didn't lose anybody we tried to keep," Cignetti said. "I think it speaks volumes to the culture and direction of the program."

IU 'SCRAMBLES THE JETS' WHEN BLUE BLOODS CIRCLED THE STAFF

When Indiana president Pam Whitten crossed paths with defensive coordinator Bryant Haines after the 2024 season, she pulled him aside for a brief chat. The conversation came at a time when his name was being floated as a candidate for several prominent job openings.

Whitten simply wanted Haines to know how much the school valued his contributions to IU's historic season. Haines was a finalist for the Broyles Award as the architect of a Hoosiers defense that ranked No. 2 in total defense (256.3 yards) and No. 6 in scoring defense (15.6 points).

It wasn't long before Indiana announced a new contract for Haines — the second in as many months — that made him one of only a handful of coordinators in the Big Ten making $2 million a year.

"He's done pretty well for himself," Cignetti said with a laugh.

It's a far cry from Cignetti only being able to offer Haines a $7,000 salary to be his defensive line coach at Indiana University of Pennsylvania in 2014.

"It was a part-time salary for a full-time job," Cignetti said. "He was at a different level than the other guys I had, yet he's not making anything."

They have maintained an open dialogue since Cignetti fended off Lafayette to keep Haines on his IUP staff for another season by combining two part-time salaries to double his pay.

"Everyone has an agent, and agents make money when they place guys in new jobs," Cignetti said. "They are always trying to move guys, and there's opportunities when you do good. He's always up front about what's going on, who is calling, we'll talk about the plusses and minuses."

At the same time, athletic director Scott Dolson was "scrambling the jets" to make sure IU had the resources to keep Haines in the fold.

The athletic department was proactive by locking Cignetti and the entire returning coaching staff to new deals before they even traveled to South Bend for the CFP game, but Dolson didn't hesitate to revisit those freshly signed contracts.

"We have to adapt to the market conditions as they change," Dolson said. "Resources aren't unlimited, but it's up to us to work together from an administrative standpoint and put resources in the right places so we can retain a coach who is super important to our program.

"It's an ongoing, day-to-day thing, particularly in the offseason when movement happens quickly and you try to

The Indiana athletic department provided the resources for Curt Cignetti to fight off overtures from traditional college football powers when it came to his roster and coaching staff. RICH JANZARUK/HERALD-TIMES

figure out what we need."

They went through the same process in May when Southern Cal pursued Owings. Cignetti long had credited Owings, who he described as a "cutting edge" staffer, for laying the foundation for success going back to their time together at James Madison.

The Hoosiers upped Owings' salary to $925,000 — a $290,000 raise — as part of a new three-year deal.

Cignetti and Dolson underlined the support they received throughout the offseason at the university level. The conversation Whitten had with Haines was an extension of her commitment to building a perennial title contender in football.

"We use the word alignment a lot," Dolson said, "and maybe it gets overused, but we are really on the same page."

It all added up to a historic financial commitment to Cignetti's coaching staff totaling $8.1 million, up from $5.9 million in 2024 and $4.7 million in 2023.

There were only five teams in the Big Ten last year with an assistant salary pool that topped $7 million (Ohio State, Michigan, Oregon, Iowa and Washington), per USA Today Sports' coaching salary database.

"The financial implications to all these deals are important," Dolson said, "but when it's all equal I think people want to go where they can be happy and feel like they are growing. I give coach Cig a ton of credit, and that was a part of the hiring process that was impressive to me — he's had so many people stay with him. The culture he creates and the way he treats people." ■

NO. 19 INDIANA 27, OLD DOMINION 14
AUGUST 30, 2025 • BLOOMINGTON, INDIANA

A VERY MIXED BAG

HOOSIERS SHOWED SOME GOOD, SOME BAD IN UNEVEN SEASON OPENER

BY GREGG DOYEL

The punt is bouncing inside the 20, the 15, the 10. One more thing going wrong for Indiana football, you know? This is the first game for the 2025 Indiana Hoosiers, against a mediocre Old Dominion team from the mediocre Sun Belt, and they've already given up a touchdown on the first play from scrimmage. The Hoosiers' offense then fails to score on four plays from the ODU 1 — three runs and a pass, then it's Old Dominion's ball — and loses a fumble on their next possession.

Well, last season was a thrill, wasn't it? New Indiana football coach Curt Cignetti comes to town and juts out his chest and talks big, and next thing you know the Hoosiers are in the 2024 College Football Playoff first rou—

Wait, what's he doing?

The punt, remember? It's an Old Dominion punt, and after IU returner Jonathan Brady decides not to catch it in the air, it's bouncing toward the goal line with a host of ODU special teamers in pursuit. One of them will down this thing inside the 5, maybe even inside the 1, and the first quarter will be just about over, and this sure feels like a potential disaste—

What is he doing?

Brady is watching the ball bounce toward him, inside the 10, and he's not getting out of the way. He's watching the football skid low along the turf, watching it get closer, closer, and at the perfect moment — the only moment this can happen — the ball takes one of those nice, pleasant bounces high into the air. It's just sitting there, and Brady's just standing there, so he decides: OK, I'll grab it.

Next thing you know, Brady is running away from the ODU pursuit — he's fast, and they weren't expecting this — and then he's getting to the sideline, and now he has a convoy of blockers. He goes 91 yards, and Memorial Stadium is rocking. This game is just sitting there, and the Hoosiers are just standing there, but now they make a decision:

OK, we'll grab it.

Shrug.

The bison mascot was cool, though. Parachuted onto the field. Highlight of the day.

CURT CIGNETTI ISN'T HAPPY WITH IU FOOTBALL

Cignetti is seething over there on the sideline, giving that 10-mile stare he gives when he cannot believe — cannot understand — what his players are doing.

"I'm not pleased with the way we played," Cignetti told reporters afterward. "Can't be any more clear than that."

Hey, Mr. and Ms. IU football fans: You think you're unhappy? Imagine being Cignetti, who saw almost everything go right a year ago in his first season in Bloomington. A year later, so much went wrong in the 2025 opener. Yes, of course, Indiana beat Old Dominion — final score: 27-14 — but that was never really in doubt.

Same goes for the Hoosiers' next two games, also at home, also against outmatched nonconference opponents: Kennesaw State and Indiana State. The Hoosiers will be 3-0 entering their fourth game, also at home, against No. 12 Illinois.

Can Cignetti's Hoosiers beat the Illini? Depends how much progress they make between now and then. The IU team that showed up Saturday afternoon probably can't beat Illinois, or many other Big Ten teams. The Hoosiers on Saturday allowed ODU quarterback Colton Joseph, whose scouting report reads like so — mediocre passer, dangerous runner — to go undetected on the read option on the first

Senior wide receiver Jonathan Brady, a transfer from California, races to the end zone on a 91-yard punt return late in the first quarter with Indiana's first points of the season. Old Dominion led 7-0 at the time. RICH JANZARUK/HERALD-TIMES

INDIANA
0
INDIANA
36

play of the game. Joseph faked a handoff on a sweep left, and every IU defender in the vicinity fell for it.

So there goes Joseph, untouched, 75 yards for a touchdown. Then it happened again. This time it was the fourth quarter, after the Hoosiers had scored 27 consecutive points. Order seemed to have been restored. The IU offense had its struggles, sure, but this was the first game, right? Teams improve the most from Week 1 to Week 2. The IU offense, with a new quarterback, will improve next week. The IU defense improved immediately after that first play — a fluke, looked like — by learning from its mistake and stifling the Monarchs. The Hoosiers led 27-7 with about seven minutes left, the crowd morphing from frustrated to mostly bored.

"You thought the rout could be on," Cignetti said. "But it wasn't."

This time, Joseph fakes a handoff up the middle, and every IU defender in the vicinity falls for it. So there goes Joseph, untouched until he crossed the goal line, 78 yards for a touchdown to make it 27-14.

Now it all looks different, doesn't it? The IU defense didn't learn from its mistake. And if the defense can allow that to happen twice — fluke has just left the chat — then maybe we should take a closer look at the IU offense. Scoring 27 points, total, against an Old Dominion team that went 5-7 last season and isn't expected to be any better this season? That's disappointing.

Scoring 27 points, total, against an ODU team that allowed an average of 28 points a game last season? And seven of those points came, as we mentioned, on a punt return? That's alarming.

"Everybody in this organization realizes we need to get better," Cignetti said. "That's just a flat-out fact."

CAN IU FOOTBALL COME CLOSE TO 2024 SUCCESS?

To be fair, not to mention putting things into context:

The 2025 Hoosiers have a lot in common with last year's 11-2 bunch: More newcomers (53 this season) than almost anyone in the country, more transfers (24) than almost everyone, more older players (29 players in their final year of eligibility) than almost everyone — and a new quarterback (California transfer Fernando Mendoza) with a promising track record.

It takes time, putting together a puzzle like this. A year ago, it took Cignetti one week. After an uninspiring 31-7 victory at home against Florida International in the opener, the Hoosiers beat Western Illinois 77-3, then beat UCLA 42-14, and then it was sunshine and rainbows until Columbus, Ohio, in late November.

How long will it take this season? Cignetti has two more easy weeks, and then it gets real.

Points of concern, beyond the IU defense's inability to stop Old Dominion from doing the only thing it does well? The offense in the red zone. The quarterback. Those are only marginally related.

The offensive line did a fine job in the middle of the field, but near the goal line the Big Ten Hoosiers couldn't make holes against the Sun Belt Monarchs. IU returns three starting linemen and has highly regarded transfers in the other two spots, but Old Dominion's front dominated inside the 10. In the Hoosiers' six trips inside the 10, they scored two touchdowns, kicked two field goals and turned it over twice on downs. Another drive ended in the red zone, on the 20, when the Hoosiers fumbled.

The Hoosiers squandered another touchdown when Omar Cooper Jr. dropped what would have been a 55-yard TD in the second quarter. IU could've — should've — scored more than 50 points. Maybe they will, in similar circumstances, in the next few weeks.

But Mendoza is going to have to get a lot better. Or maybe just play like he did at Cal, where he holds the career record for completion percentage (66.4%) and threw for 3,004 yards and 16 touchdowns in 11 games last season. He completed 68.7% of his passes last season.

Saturday, Mendoza was 18-for-31 — that's 58.1% — for 193 yards and no touchdowns. True, the drop by Cooper hurt his final numbers. Also true: Mendoza had a handful of throws that could've or even should've been intercepted. But Old Dominion isn't very good, so Mendoza got away with it.

Old Dominion isn't very good, so the Hoosiers won this game. They'll win the next two as well. Illinois visits Sept. 20. They've got a ways to go, to win that one. ■

California transfer Fernando Mendoza, a 6-foot-5, 225-pound redshirt junior, looks to pass against Old Dominion. Indiana's new starting quarterback completed 18 of 31 passes for 193 yards in his Hoosiers debut. RICH JANZARUK/HERALD-TIMES

INDIANA

OPERATION BIGFOOT

HOW HOOSIER THE BISON CAME BACK TO ROAM THE SIDELINES

BY ZACH OSTERMAN

For Christmas in 2024, Scott Dolson's children gifted Indiana's athletic director something nearly no one else would understand.

A clapperboard — the black-and-white apparatus snapped together to signify the start of filming on a movie set — with the words "Operation Bigfoot" written on the production line.

The clapperboard sits on Dolson's desk. Sharp-eyed viewers could have spotted it in the background of a video posted to IU's social media channels in May. Because that was when Operation Bigfoot went off, and Indiana brought back the bison as its mascot.

The idea of a mascot steadily gained traction with Indiana fans in recent years. And Hoosier the Bison made its long-awaited debut before Indiana's season opener against Old Dominion. The new mascot arrived in style: parachuting into Memorial Stadium, trailing an IU flag and executing a pinpoint landing at the 10-yard line.

As the crowd went wild, the mascot pumped its arms to further fire up the fans while crossing the field. Hoosier the Bison hustled into a tunnel only to reemerge riding a motorcycle. After a seamless parking job, the mascot jumped and pumped to more cheering as a new era dawned with an old idea.

ONCE UPON A TIME, A BISON ROAMED MEMORIAL STADIUM

For a little more than a century, Indiana's athletic teams have gone by "Hoosiers," a term meant to refer to a native of the state whose origins have long been debated and almost certainly cannot be historically proven. While "Hoosiers" embodies a certain cultural resonance for IU fans, it's hard to assign a physical manifestation to a word with no universally agreed-upon meaning.

Decades ago, for just a few years, drawing on the animal figuring prominently on the state seal, IU tried a bison mascot. It was introduced in 1965 and pretty much abandoned by the end of that decade.

But it never really went away. Nick's English Hut pound jars still feature a bison image. Fans produced AI-generated graphics depicting an IU bison on social media. "Bring back the bison" became a rallying cry stretching from podcasts like the popular CrimsonCast to independent retail, including the popular Indianapolis-based company Homefield Apparel.

Athletic officials felt that groundswell, which came to a head in December 2024 when IU Student Government passed its Bring Back the Bison Act reinstating the bison as the university's official mascot. From that point forward, the athletic department was in.

"The students really pushing it was a big determining factor," said Jeremy Gray, IU senior associate athletic director for strategic communications. "It was clear the fan base had really rallied behind the idea."

Department officials settled on the code name Operation Bigfoot as a way to talk about the mascot introduction in official correspondence while sidestepping premature attention. Dolson firmly supported the idea.

Last year's football success, which included Indiana's first Saturday visit from ESPN's "College GameDay," brought into relief the value of an identifiable mascot. When legendary "GameDay" analyst (and former IU coach) Lee Corso picked the Hoosiers to beat Washington, Indiana had no

After an absence of several decades, fan momentum and student government's Bring Back the Bison Act helped resurrect Indiana's bison mascot. The athletic department did the rest and capitalized on bison merchandise. RICH JANZARUK/HERALD-TIMES

ION

mascot headgear for him to pull on as was his custom. Corso opted instead for a hat commemorating his team's 1979 Holiday Bowl victory over BYU.

"Finding something to represent the school in those large, public ways," Gray said, "I think it became obvious a mascot could help with that."

The department met with student groups, including Student Government and IU's Board of Aeons — a student advisory group that works closely with the university president — to discuss ways to introduce the bison to the student body.

IU began subtly implanting bison imagery across its branding with small logos in the corners of video scoreboard graphics and horns crashing through schedule posters for the 2025-26 athletic year.

"We decided to lean into it," Gray said.

THE EXISTENTIAL QUESTION: LIVE ANIMAL OR A COSTUME

A variety of considerations went into the selection and design of Hoosier the Bison.

Concerns over staffing, upkeep and animal welfare steered the department away from a live mascot to the more common option of a person in a costume.

IU knew from the outset it wanted a mascot muscular and imposing enough to project a robust image of the department. Able, as Gray put it, "to win a play fight against a turtle."

But also one that was approachable and endearing to children. Enter graduating senior Adam Day, who last spring built one of his final projects as a student around studying mascots over time. Working alongside department officials, he found the key to giving mascots personal appeal lay in their eyes. Specifically, they needed to be soft and sympathetic, rather than hard or empty.

The department engaged Alinco Costumes in Utah, a company with a history of designing mascots or characters for professional baseball, football and basketball franchises, as well as corporations such as Nestle and Disney. Its website claims credit for more than half of the NBA's team mascots.

Mark Skirvin, senior assistant athletic director for marketing, worked with Alinco through several rough sketches before settling on a design. And thus, Hoosier was born.

He still needed an announcement. Operation Bigfoot went to studio.

Gray, a self-professed cinephile, drew inspiration from several movies for a series of videos released over several days in May on IU's social media channels.

Gray's own character, Ray, opening a glowing box in the first video nodded to "Pulp Fiction" and "Raiders of the Lost Ark." Recent basketball player Sydney Parrish assumed a role akin to Sigourney Weaver's Ripley, from the "Alien" series, in discovering evidence of a large, unidentifiable creature.

In total, the department also included nods to films including "ET," "Silence of the Lambs," "Scream," "Jurassic Park," "Return of the Jedi," the Marvel series and "The Usual Suspects."

The final shot of the mascot standing, back to camera, atop the Memorial Stadium press box drew from the final scene in "The Last of the Mohicans."

When IU approached coach Curt Cignetti about a Roy Schneider-inspired "Jaws" scene, he replied, "Nah, I've got what I want to say." In his cameo, Cignetti watches film when the silhouette of a bison head appears behind him. Cignetti turns and says simply, "Where you been?" ■

Above: Hoosier the Bison has no trouble adapting to his new home in Memorial Stadium. RICH JANZARUK/HERALD-TIMES

Opposite: Hoosier the Bison makes a triumphant return in dramatic fashion by parachuting into Memorial Stadium before the opener. Later, Hoosier drove a motorcycle around the field. RICH JANZARUK/HERALD-TIMES

TEAM
FASTRAX

NO. 21 INDIANA 56, KENNESAW STATE 9
SEPTEMBER 6, 2025 • BLOOMINGTON, INDIANA

A FAMILY AFFAIR

MENDOZA BROTHERS NOW FIRST DUO IN DECADE TO THROW A TD IN SAME GAME

BY MICHAEL NIZIOLEK

Fernando Mendoza's frustration over coming out of the game in the middle of a drive gave way to joy as he watched his younger brother Alberto throw for his first career touchdown in the final minutes of Indiana's 56-9 destruction of Kennesaw State.

After Alberto connected with receiver Charlie Becker on a fade route for the 6-yard score, Fernando ran down the sidelines to celebrate with a leaping chest bump.

They become the first set of brothers to throw touchdown passes in the same game for the same team since 2015 when Brandon and Austin Allen accomplished the feat for Arkansas against Tennessee-Martin.

"It was fantastic," said Fernando, who earlier had thrown four TD passes. "I want to give all the glory to God on that. That was amazing to be here with him and have that partnership that we're working together, trying to push each other to get better and get the Hoosiers as many wins as possible."

Fernando was so locked into the game — even with a 49-9 lead — he didn't realize that his departure would present an opportunity for his brother. Fernando might have finished the drive if he didn't scramble on a first down and open himself up to a big hit.

Kennesaw State defensive back Alexander Ford sent Fernando flying into his teammates on the sidelines and was flagged for unnecessary roughness. Mendoza ran for 13 yards on the play.

As Indiana got ready to line up at Kennesaw State's 15, coach Curt Cignetti made the switch with a little more than eight minutes left to play.

"As a competitor, for a split second, I was like I want to score again," Fernando said with a smile. "Then I realized my little brother was going in."

It was a special moment for the brothers, who were teammates at Christopher Columbus High School in Miami. Alberto, two years younger, followed his brother as Columbus' quarterback and won two state championships. Fernando was the backup QB as a sophomore on a state championship team. Alberto posted bigger career numbers at Christopher Columbus than Fernando: 4,596 yards and 57 TDs versus 2,222 yards and 29 TDs.

Alberto pushed for the Hoosiers to land the California transfer even though he knew it would push him down the depth chart. Fernando was familiar with IU's staffers when he entered the transfer portal in December because they had recruited Alberto while coaching at James Madison.

"We do everything together," Fernando said during spring practice. "We watch film together, we get better together, we have tough times together. It's been great, and he's been a steppingstone to me learning the offense."

Alberto got a taste of game action while redshirting as a freshman in 2024. He played two drives in a 77-3 victory over Western Illinois, but he was mostly in the game to hand the ball off and run out the clock. He did complete his only pass, a 6-yarder, and rushed twice for a 5-yard loss and a 2-yard gain (on fourth-and-goal from the WIU 7).

He did get to kneel on the game's final play.

Alberto got a few more opportunities to showcase his skill set against Kennesaw State (0-2). After his TD pass with 6:03 left, the Owls went three-and-out, and Alberto started another drive from his 17 with 3:54 left. He drained the clock with 12-yard and 17-yard completions for first downs and took a knee at midfield.

"To see him out there and operate efficiently with confidence and no hesitation is great," Fernando said. "It really shows he's going to be able to take the next step and be a great quarterback one day."

Indiana's Alberto Mendoza (16) and Fernando Mendoza (15) celebrate Alberto's first career touchdown pass, a 6-yarder to Charlie Becker with 6:30 left in the fourth quarter. Fernando earlier had thrown four TD passes, equaling his career high. RICH JANZARUK/HERALD-TIMES

MENDOZA-TO-SARRATT COMBO STRIKES PAY DIRT THREE TIMES

After his less than eye-popping performance in the opener, Fernando Mendoza filled the stat sheet against Kennesaw State and established a connection with Elijah Sarratt, his all-conference wide receiver.

Mendoza threw for four touchdowns for the first time in his career, completing 18 of 25 passes for 245 yards with no interceptions or sacks. His scoring strikes covered nine, three and 20 yards to Sarratt, he found Omar Cooper Jr. for a 40-yard completion and he ran three times for 20 yards.

Mendoza acknowledged he needed to look for Sarratt more often after a five-target, three-catch game in the opener. The player whose teammates call him Waffle House because — like the popular greasy spoon chain — he's always open gained 97 yards with nine catches on 13 targets.

"Fantastic," Mendoza said. "He's Waffle House."

Cignetti compared Mendoza's improvement from week to week with Kurtis Rouke's in 2024.

"All these new quarterbacks, they build on their successes early in the season," Cignetti said. "You win, they play well, they build on it. Same thing happened last year with Kurtis. He didn't have the greatest opener. He sure played good the second game even though the opponent (was Western Illinois). And obviously lights out the third." ■

— Zach Osterman contributed.

NO. 19 INDIANA 73, INDIANA STATE 0
SEPTEMBER 12, 2025 • BLOOMINGTON, INDIANA

DOMINATION AND ANTICIPATION

INDIANA SETS HOME WINNING STREAK RECORD, AWAITS TOUGH ILLINI

BY ZACH OSTERMAN

Indiana's unceremonious 73-0 dismissal of Indiana State on a Friday night ensured for the No. 19 Hoosiers a perfect nonconference season that should never have been anything else. Now, ninth-ranked Illinois comes into view, and with it the chance to find out what this team can do.

The inherent strangeness of these last three weeks had been in watching a fan base so unfamiliar with anticipation learning how to be patient.

It's not that IU fans never looked forward to a moment. It's that they had, historically, few moments to look forward to, at least ones of this magnitude. It would be the first meeting of top-20 teams at Memorial Stadium since Oct. 24, 1987, when the 15th-ranked Hoosiers beat No. 20 Michigan 14-10 on homecoming. IU hasn't beaten a top-10 team at home since taking down No. 3 Purdue 19-14 on Nov. 25, 1967.

Which handed Curt Cignetti an enviable problem:

His team's ambitions were clear. The Hoosiers' talent may well be College Football Playoff-caliber again in 2025. But how do you keep the main thing the main thing — as Cignetti likes to say — when what lies just beyond it is so tantalizing?

It was in the answer to that question, delivered by Indiana's performance Friday night, that Cignetti took greatest comfort. Even with arguably the biggest home game in living memory waiting just beyond the horizon, for 60 minutes against Indiana State (2-1), he stalked a sideline that never lost its focus, its intensity, its energy, its commitment to the task at hand.

"I expected us to have a dominant performance, and we did," Cignetti said. "I didn't see anybody relaxing at any point in the game."

The Hoosiers have won all 11 home games since Cignetti took over in 2024. They had won 10 straight at home only once, under Bill Mallory from 1987-88. The next longest streaks were seven games (1967-68 and 1991-92).

Records were matched, records were broken, career bests were set. Names like Cooper (Omar, 207 yards, four touchdowns) and Mendoza (Fernando, 19 of 20 passing, best single-game completion rate in program history) were carved into IU's record book.

Cignetti and his staff will have been just as pleased to see another dominant display from a defensive front that, after being challenged following the Old Dominion victory, turned out 30 punishing tackles for loss across the last two games.

Even adjusted for the competition, those are commanding numbers. They reflect the potential for Indiana to be as disruptive and impactful at the line of scrimmage as the Hoosiers were last year, yet another encouraging sign when line play underscored so much of IU's defensive success in 2024.

"We want to come out there and attack the line of scrimmage and win the line of scrimmage in every game," said Tyrique Taylor, a redshirt junior defensive tackle. "We felt really good about it, but we've still got to work."

Cignetti and his staff also should feel better about their depth behind center, having watched Alberto Mendoza toss two touchdown passes in relief of his brother in the second half. They were valuable snaps for a young quarterback history tells us Indiana would need at some point this fall.

And then there was the main man, the elder Mendoza. Completing his first 14 passes. Swapping his advanced chemistry with Elijah Sarratt last week for record-breaking connections with Cooper. Throwing for five touchdowns. ■

Fernando Mendoza filled the stat sheet with five TD passes (a career high), a .950 completion percentage (a school record), a rushing touchdown (a 7-yarder 3½ minutes into the game) and 270 passing yards (despite sitting out the second half). RICH JANZARUK/HERALD-TIMES

INDIANA
15
B1G

NO. 17 INDIANA 63, NO. 8 ILLINOIS 10
SEPTEMBER 20, 2025 • BLOOMINGTON, INDIANA

BETTER BELIEVE IT

IU MAKES BIG TEN HISTORY, PROVES CIGNETTI'S HOOSIERS ARE HERE TO STAY

BY ZACH OSTERMAN

The skies opened unexpectedly in the second half Saturday night, unloading a sheeting late September rain across 56,088 delirious souls.

The damp, wet summer had in recent weeks given way to a dry meteorological fall, the grass only just beginning to brown for the first time all year. The last three days had been Bloomington's hottest in weeks. The rain was finally welcome.

It sent a few hundred people for the exits, but many thousands more that made up one of the largest crowds in Memorial Stadium history stayed. Illuminated by floodlights, connected through unrestrained joy, they waved towels and soaked T-shirts over their heads, belting out the lyrics to The Killers' "Mr. Brightside" with the reckless abandon of a mob handed the opportunity to suspend doubt for one night, and believe that anything might be possible.

At the end of No. 17 Indiana's historic undressing of No. 8 Illinois — final score, 63-10 — those thousands of fans danced their way out into the cool Indiana night, their happiness a warning to the rest of college football: Now you're gonna believe in IU football, whether you like it or not.

"You guys control all that stuff," coach Curt Cignetti said, refusing to be drawn into discussions of that narrative. "I've just gotta get them ready. And then we all play our games and see where it shakes out at the end of the year."

Last season, Cignetti wouldn't have been so demure. Last season, with a jaded fan base and a surging team and a skeptical sport, Cignetti was the King of College Football Quotes. He rolled through them like peak Steve Spurrier — "Purdue sucks," "Google me" and, of course, "We're the emerging superpower in college football."

Cignetti said those things when and how he did because he knew he had to invigorate those fans. He had to inject arrogance and self-belief into a program history said deserved neither.

"I know I stirred things up last year media-wise, because I felt I had to," Cignetti said. "This place, the fan base was dead and (we) needed to set some expectations."

None of that needed on this Saturday night. Words paled in comparison to the cold, hard reality Indiana laid on Bret Bielema's team.

The Hoosiers (4-0, 1-0 Big Ten) outgained the Illinois by 418 yards. They sacked Illini quarterbacks seven times and held the ball for nearly 40 of the 60 minutes.

Fernando Mendoza — who passed for 267 yards and five touchdowns — finished with as many incompletions (two) as Illinois did team yards rushing.

Illinois (3-1, 0-1) entered this game with more hype. More expectation. Not just a higher ranking but greater national respect, best illustrated by the sheer number of pundits picking the Illini to win.

If anything, this was meant to be Illinois' crowning moment. Winners of 10 games last season, the Illini were thrown around through the offseason as "this year's Indiana," a suggestion that they might be the next upstart Big Ten playoff team. The summer darling of an autumn sport.

Cignetti and his team left that hype in the July heat — and Illinois in a heap of proverbial ash on the visiting sideline.

E.J. Williams Jr. skies for an 11-yard touchdown in the second quarter that gave the Hoosiers a 21-7 lead over Illinois. It was the second of Fernando Mendoza's five TD passes, which tied his career high set a week earlier. RICH JANZARUK/HERALD-TIMES

"At a loss for words," Bielema told reporters. "I've never been a part of anything like that."

IU fans of a certain vintage might remind Bielema he had, just wearing the shoe on the other foot.

It was Bielema's Wisconsin team in 2010 that laid 83 points on Indiana in Bill Lynch's final season. Two years later, his Badgers beat IU 62-14 at Bloomington, in a game billed by a curious set of circumstances as an unlikely route to the Big Ten title game for the Hoosiers.

Results like this used to happen to Indiana, not the other way around. That as much as anything is the measure of the excellence of Cignetti's work these last 22 months. He has turned America's losingest program into a merciless winner, and the sport's most cynical, broken fan base into a congregation of absolute believers.

It is virtually impossible, if you haven't spent time around this program at its worst, to understand what it feels like now at its best.

In a space of time that backdropped against the wide context of history seems almost overnight, Cignetti has turned Indiana football into something approximating what he said it was last November: The emerging superpower in college football.

That will remain a stretch until the Hoosiers do some more serious winning. But let's be fair, there's not much that's more serious than this. Saturday was hardly the first time Cignetti had taken an old Indiana bully out behind the barn.

But this was different. This was not Indiana riding the crest of a wave across an uncommonly easy schedule, bashing its way through overmatched and overawed opponents simply incapable of, in the space of a few days, matching anything like IU's newfound swagger.

College football circled this game in April. It was the talk of at the Big Ten's media days in July. In a world less driven by the politics of television partnerships, all the big pregame shows would have been posted up around Memorial Stadium at sunrise Saturday morning.

Indiana snuck up on nothing and no one in this game. Illinois had weeks, if not months, to prepare, and for whatever trouble it went to, Bielema's team got undressed historically.

Cignetti left the loud part unsaid when, at the end of that quote about seeing where it shakes out, he grinned and looked at Jeff Keag, his sports information director.

"I want to," he said, smiling wider, "but I'm not."

There would be no viral comments on this night. His team's performance made the loudest statement possible. Before Saturday night, the most points a Big Ten team had scored against an Associated Press top-10 opponent was 62. That distinction belonged to Ohio State. That's who and what Indiana supplanted when it did what it did.

And the warning attached to that kind of achievement rang treble loud and crystal clear across college football, as stadiums emptied and fans drove home, and Saturday became Sunday: Indiana isn't going anywhere. ■

Above: Tight end Riley Nowakowski, in his first year with Indiana after five with Wisconsin, celebrates his 43-yard TD catch. RICH JANZARUK/HERALD-TIMES

Opposite: Kellen Wyatt, Indiana's leading edge rusher, lets out a primal scream after sacking Illini quarterback Luke Altmyer. The Hoosiers sacked Altmyer seven times for 47 yards in losses. Wyatt's season ended a month later because of a knee injury. RICH JANZARUK/HERALD-TIMES

INDIANA
13

B1G

QUARTERBACK

15 FERNANDO MENDOZA

PREP COACH BEGGED FOR COLLEGES TO RECRUIT THE TALL QB; NOW HE'S A HEISMAN CONTENDER

BY ZACH OSTERMAN | SEPTEMBER 25, 2025

Once, during his recruitment out of Miami Columbus High School, Fernando Mendoza traveled north to an ACC campus in search of a scholarship offer.

The Explorers' long, strong-armed quarterback was a serial winner for a serially winning program in south Florida. Staff after staff would make its way through Columbus — the school's rich football history counts three state titles and an alumni list that includes Brian Griese, Mario Cristobal, Mike Shula, C.J. Henderson and Joaquin Gonzalez — where coach Dave Dunn would beg them to look at his quarterback.

Watch how he leads. Catalogue the variety of ways he makes plays. Offer this kid a place at your school.

No one stepped up. It was, Dunn said, "one of the most frustrating things I've ever been through in my life."

He won't say now which school invited Mendoza to come throw at that offseason camp, only that the trip required a flight so it couldn't have been Mendoza's hometown Hurricanes. After a typically impressive performance, the coach recruiting Mendoza at said unnamed school offered him a five-word missive: Have a nice flight home.

Dunn thinks about that episode regularly now, with his former signal caller leading America in touchdown passes and rocketing up lists of Heisman favorites leading Indiana football's offense. He said he's considered sending an email to all the coaches who passed Mendoza over, laying out the receipts all of college football can now read.

"I have not done that and I will not do that," Dunn said, "but I want to do that."

But Dunn — whose resume includes stops at San Diego, Indiana State, Harvard, Florida Atlantic, Marshall and two Division III schools as head coach — will confess to some self-satisfaction, watching Mendoza thrive at Indiana and expose all those faulty evaluations from a time in his career when so many schools failed to recognize Mendoza's tremendous potential.

"(Coaches) call me now," Dunn said, "like, 'Boy, we screwed that one up.'"

A STRONG MENDOZA FAMILY LEGACY

Fernando Mendoza V grew up in a football family. His father, Fernando Mendoza IV, played with Cristobal (now Miami coach) at Columbus. Fernando's little brother, Alberto, also quarterbacked Columbus, winning back-to-back state titles before signing with Curt Cignetti at IU.

The Mendoza brothers grew up sharing a bedroom, a position and a sport, with a father and eventually a high school coach who gave them the tough-love mentorship that made them FBS quarterbacks in the first place.

"There were times we were probably bad cop, bad cop. We'd be tough on both boys," Dunn said. "But that's how they want to be coached. That's how they're wired. Both of those guys, they don't want someone to tell them everyone's going to be OK."

Dunn appreciated something else about Fernando Mendoza IV.

A former lineman, he handed both his sons a different perspective on offense. He pushed them as much as they

Fernando Mendoza's advocates were vindicated with his spectacular season at Indiana. In December and January, Mendoza received numerous awards, including the Grange-Griffin Trophy as the MVP of the Big Ten title game. GRACE HOLLARS/INDYSTAR

wanted to be pushed. And he always walked in lockstep with their coach.

"You hear all these parent stories," Dunn said. "Their father never bothered me about anything. Whatever I would say, he would back me."

The results remain difficult to argue with.

Fernando Mendoza passed for 2,222 yards and 29 touchdowns across parts of two seasons as Columbus' starter, his tenure interrupted by the COVID-19 pandemic, and he won a state title as the Explorers' No. 2 in 2019.

Alberto Mendoza took the wheel when his brother left for college, passing for 4,596 yards and 57 touchdowns, with a pair of state titles and two Class 4 Metro Florida Player of the Year honors on his CV.

But while Alberto Mendoza's recruitment unfolded with relative ease — he committed to Cignetti at James Madison before flipping to IU after Cignetti moved to Bloomington — Dunn struggled to understand why he couldn't get college coaches to buy into the Mendozas' elder son.

Frustrating as it was then, for the player and his coach, Dunn said he believes now those setbacks better prepared Fernando Mendoza for the stage onto which he now strides.

"He works so hard at it, and he's such a good kid," Dunn said. "For those two reasons alone, you want him to have success."

FERNANDO MENDOZA CONTINUES PROVING DOUBTERS WRONG

Whatever adversity his recruitment posed, Mendoza, who's 6-feet-5, 225 pounds, seized the earliest opportunity presented him to prove his doubters wrong.

He signed with Cal, the highest-profile program on an offer list that eventually also included Bryant, Lehigh, Penn, Yale and hometown Florida International. After redshirting his first season in Berkeley, Mendoza won the starting job behind center midway through his second.

From that point forward, his trajectory has remained pointed firmly upward.

He started 19 of the 20 games in which he appeared for the Bears, leading Cal to consecutive bowl berths. When he left Berkeley at the end of last season, he did so the program's all-time leader in completion percentage, having thrown for 30 touchdowns to just 16 interceptions, and more than 4,700 yards.

That success positioned Mendoza among the best quarterbacks in his class when he entered the transfer portal in December. Georgia, Missouri and hometown Miami all reached out.

So did Indiana, a program into which Fernando Mendoza had uncommon insight. Alberto had just completed his freshman season (as a redshirt) in Bloomington, a historic one for the Hoosiers. He did not press his older brother for a commitment, but rather offered what Mendoza described in a January interview with IndyStar as "great" perspective on IU football.

Fernando Mendoza coupled that to the success Cignetti and his staff had shown adapting transfer quarterbacks into their offense, when he committed on Christmas Eve 2024. He did not want for recruiting attention his second time through the process, but Fernando Mendoza didn't have to look far afield for his next home.

"I still believe I have a ton of things to get better at," Mendoza said during that January phone call. "I just thought, 'This is a great situation.'"

FERNANDO MENDOZA, 'THE GUY FROM DAY 1'

After his commitment, Fernando Mendoza grabbed his brother's playbook and started cramming.

He arrived to Bloomington knowing he would be expected to contribute right away, and never hid from that pressure.

"At Cal, I was there for three years, and the past two years, I was a team captain," he said during spring camp. "I'm expected to be the guy from Day 1. It's a great challenge, one I've accepted."

Cignetti pushed Mendoza in the ways Mendoza expected — with the same demanding approach the Mendoza brothers got in high school. IU's second-year coach suggested by the end of spring camp he'd seen his new quarterback begin to properly settle in.

As a rule, Cignetti doesn't name team captains. And he's not big on labeling players as starters. But through spring, summer and into fall, he also never made any secret of who his No. 1 quarterback was, or what he expected of him.

"He's got a quick whip, strong arm, accurate, mobile," Cignetti said earlier this year. "The biggest thing when he came to us was working with him in the pocket and the drop-back game, being a little bit more patient, poised going through his progressions."

After a modest opener against Old Dominion — one reflecting some of those adjustments and improvements

Fernando Mendoza fit in and became a leader quickly upon arriving at Indiana on his way to making history with the Hoosiers. He had been a captain at California for two seasons. RICH JANZARUK/HERALD-TIMES

Cignetti listed — Fernando Mendoza has sprinted to the front of college football's conscious mind.

Through the first four games of the season, he's second in the Big Ten in both completion percentage and passer rating. His 14 touchdown passes lead the FBS, and he's one of just three quarterbacks with a double-digit touchdown total and no interceptions.

No performance spoke so loudly as Saturday, when Mendoza finished 21-of-23 passing for 267 yards and five touchdowns, in a 63-10 evisceration of previously top-10-ranked Illinois. That performance, backdropped against his season, slashed Mendoza's Heisman odds and inserted him firmly into the discussion over college football's best quarterback in 2025.

"Somebody was saying he's the leader for the Heisman," Iowa coach Kirk Ferentz said. "I don't have a Heisman vote but I'd vote for him based on what I've seen."

The tests get tougher, starting this weekend in Iowa City. Ferentz runs America's most do-your-job successful program. Cignetti this week described the Hawkeyes' greatest strengths by saying simply, "They will not beat themselves."

Saturday marks Mendoza's first road game as a Hoosier, in a stadium famous for untracking ranked visitors. Then comes Oregon after the bye week, with Penn State lurking later in the schedule.

In America's richest conference, success only steepens the road.

Fernando Mendoza wanted, waited and worked for the opportunity to navigate that road. Now, it unfurls before him, as with each step forward he rises to meet it.

"He's got a tremendous upside, and he prepares," Cignetti said. "He's a tremendous person. He will do everything he can to be the best he can be. It means a lot to him. He wants to be great." ■

NO. 12 INDIANA 20, IOWA 15
SEPTEMBER 27, 2025 • IOWA CITY, IOWA

ALL THE WAY UP

IU HEADED TOWARD THE TOP OF COLLEGE FOOTBALL, LIKE MENDOZA

BY GREGG DOYEL

On the play we'll be talking about again and again, all the way into December when the 2025 Indiana football team is playing again in the College Football Playoff, Iowa is coming after quarterback Fernando Mendoza with everything it's got. And Iowa's got a lot, eight defenders near the line of scrimmage, every last one of them bearing down on No. 15 in that creamy #iufb uniform.

Apparently, Iowa hasn't been paying attention, because Fernando Mendoza isn't afraid. Hadn't we seen that all game? I'm thinking about the time when ... well, let's return to that a little later, because at the moment Mendoza is standing in the pocket, and Iowa has more players attacking the quarterback than IU has defending it.

Mendoza is about to earn the trip to New York City he'll take later this season for the Heisman presentation.

Did I just say IU quarterback Fernando Mendoza will win the 2025 Heisman Trophy? Nope. Just said he'll be at the ceremony. A finalist, at a minimum.

Anyway.

The game is tied in the final 90 seconds and the play is unfolding and Iowa is coming and Mendoza is standing there and it's the craziest thing. The Iowa pass rush is shoving the IU offensive line into Mendoza's space. He's about to be hit by two of his own players, to be followed no doubt by half the Iowa defense, and Mendoza is still standing there, waiting for Elijah Sarratt to get open.

"Waffle House," they call Sarratt — because he's open 24 hours a day, get it? — and sure enough, Sarratt flashes open on a slant pattern from Mendoza's left.

Mendoza throws the easiest, most difficult pass you ever saw, just flips the ball about 10 yards over the middle, hitting Sarratt in stride — hitting him so perfectly, Sarratt doesn't have to do anything but keep running as fast as he can. That allows him to step out of the diving tackle attempt at the Iowa 40, and now Sarratt is sprinting to the end zone and Kinnick Stadium is gasping and Sarratt is scoring the game-winning touchdown in the Hoosiers' 20-15 victory.

Back near midfield Mendoza is doing what he does, giving thanks to God above. The leader of the No. 12 IU football team holds his hands in supplication and raises them to the heavens.

CURT CIGNETTI, KIRK FERENTZ GO OLD SCHOOL

On a day the swag wasn't working for swaggy IU coach Curt Cignetti, the Hoosiers weren't going to win with magic or beauty. They weren't going to win by catching breaks, either. This was a day where game officials reviewed four bang-bang plays on instant replay, all four plays called initially in favor of the Hawkeyes. Iowa was playing at home. A coincidence, maybe. Whatever the case, the replay review upheld all four calls, all for the same team.

Ever seen that before? Me neither.

IU wasn't going to get lucky, is my point. The Hoosiers weren't going to swashbuckle their way to victory, either. Cignetti and his staff are normally daring to the point of dangerous, but on Saturday they were going for it on fourth-and-1 — twice — by running the ball up the middle. And they were being turned back both times by an Iowa run defense that came into the game ranked seventh in the country in rushing defense at 60.8 yards a game.

The IU offense came into Kinnick Stadium averaging 588.8 yards (second in the country) and 54.8 points (third),

Omar Cooper Jr. hauls in a 14-yard touchdown pass 87 seconds after the opening kickoff. The Hoosiers didn't score another touchdown until 88 seconds were left in the game. JULIA HANSEN/IOWA CITY PRESS-CITIZEN

TOGETHER
4

but Iowa coach Kirk Ferentz got the game he wanted. Slow, ugly, something very much like the 70-year-old Ferentz himself. Something out of the 1950s.

Didn't start that way, though. IU intercepted Iowa two plays into the game, then scored on a TD pass from Mendoza to Omar Cooper Jr. two plays after that. The game was 87 seconds old and the Hoosiers led 7-0, and was this going to be another 60-minute knockout, like the Hoosiers' 63-10 wipeout of No. 8 Illinois a week earlier?

In a word: No.

In another word: Ferentz.

He grimed the game up, sending his running backs and even his quarterbacks — both of them — into the line of scrimmage, and sending pass rushers into the IU offensive backfield. Iowa was beating its head against the wall that is Cignetti's team, and Iowa was making it work.

What did Cignetti do? Not what you'd expect. Actually — and someday maybe we'll remember this lesson — Cignetti did the exact opposite of what you'd expect. Rather than trying to beat Iowa's ugly ball with prettier and prettier playcalling, Cignetti and his offensive staff decided to beat *their* head against the Iowa wall.

And they decided to turn Fernando Mendoza, who is neither exceptionally fast nor strong, into a battering ram.

And Fernando Mendoza? Well, knock a lot of us over with a feather, but in the toughest game IU has had to play all season, Mendoza was one of the toughest guys on the field. You know that saying — ball don't lie?

Blood don't lie, either.

IU QUARTERBACK FERNANDO MENDOZA FOR HEISMAN

Remember earlier in the story, when I told you Mendoza isn't scared? And how I was thinking about the time when ...

This isn't the time I had in mind:

Late first half, IU at its 41 with about 15 seconds left and needing a big play to get into field-goal position. Mendoza drops back, and here comes *Iowa*. Who, in particular, for Iowa? All of them. Here comes Iowa. Mendoza stands there and throws a perfect 17-yard pass to Sarratt before Iowa crashes into him. Personal foul. Roughing the passer. Add 15 yards to the completion, and IU kicks a field goal on the next play to tie the game at 10 going into halftime.

This isn't the time I had in mind, either:

Early fourth quarter, IU at its 31, second-and-4. Mendoza drops back and then takes off. Looks like a designed QB draw, and the Hoosiers had been calling Mendoza's number all game. On this one he takes off for 6 yards, getting the first down and then getting drilled in the back by 6-foot-3, 259-pound Iowa defensive end Ethan Hurkett. Two plays later, Mendoza drops back again, and here comes Iowa. Yes, Iowa. Mendoza stands there until Waffle House, er Sarratt, gets open and hits Sarratt for 29 yards just before an Iowa defender smashes into him, running through Mendoza and smashing him in the face with a forearm.

Mendoza isn't afraid, remember? And this is the time I had in mind:

Last play of the third quarter, third-and-15 at the IU 34. Mendoza drops back, and nobody's open. Fifteen yards is a long way to run and he's not fast, OK? But he spots an opening, sees the first-down marker on the sideline and heads that way. He also sees Iowa safety Xavier Nwankpa heading there to meet him. Mendoza can peel off, gain maybe 11 or 12 yards before getting out of bounds safely, but he makes another decision:

Screw it.

In that one spot where the sideline meets the first-down marker, Mendoza meets Nwankpa and is blasted about 10 yards out of bounds. Cignetti wants a penalty — late hit, unnecessary roughness, cruelty to quarterbacks, something — but Cignetti hasn't been getting his way all day, and it doesn't start there either. No foul. Mendoza is short of the marker, and now he's bleeding from multiple spots on his right elbow.

His throwing elbow.

Despite all that abuse, Mendoza finished this game 13 of 23 for 233 yards, two touchdowns and, sure, his first interception of the season. His TD-to-INT ratio is now 16-to-1.

That's the guy Iowa tried to intimidate on the play that decided this game? Maybe all the Hawkeyes knew about Mendoza's personality were his sound bites. As he showed afterward on the Peacock telecast, Mendoza might just be the single nicest person in the world. He was using his time to thank God, thank the TV network, congratulate Iowa for the hard-fought game, commend Iowa's defense and compliment Iowa's crowd.

You know what they say about nice guys, of course. They finish last, right? We're watching Mendoza taking a velvet sledgehammer to that idea. He has Indiana heading to the top of college football, and when the Heisman Trophy is handed out on Dec. 13, he might just be walking on stage to accept it. ■

Aiden Fisher (left) and Kellan Wyatt bring down Iowa tight end DJ Vonnahme. The Indiana defense kept the game close, setting the stage for Fernando Mendoza's fourth-quarter heroics. JULIA HANSEN/IOWA CITY PRESS-CITIZEN

INDIANA
FISHER
4

COACH

CURT CIGNETTI

PRODIGY OF A HALL-OF-FAMER, CIGNETTI CLIMBED THE COACHING LADDER CONFIDENT HE KNEW THE KEYS TO BUILDING A WINNER

BY ZACH OSTERMAN | OCTOBER 5, 2025

Frank Cignetti Sr. retired where he finished coaching, Indiana, Pennsylvania. He made a home just as he had made a hall-of-fame career there, eventually watching his son, Curt, follow in his footsteps coaching the Crimson Hawks.

One day near Christmas in 2016, Curt appeared at his door. Life was good for the younger Cignetti, who just finished 10-2 with a second-straight Division II playoff appearance.

And yet, Curt had dropped by to tell his father he wouldn't be staying. Elon, then a Colonial Athletic Association school in North Carolina with a moribund football program, had moved quickly in offering its head job, and Curt accepted.

It was an unconventional move. After six years, 53 victories and three playoff berths, the son of a program legend seemed well-positioned to wait for the right next job. Surely that wasn't a small private school in a football-mad league with just six conference victories in its previous five years.

Frank Cignetti asked his son what anyone would have: "You sure you want to do that?" Curt's reply reflected the same blunt confidence that had since become recognizable as his custom.

"Dad," Curt Cignetti recalled saying, "we're going to go down there, and we're gonna kick some ass.

"And he said, 'I haven't seen you this excited in a long time.'"

College football has come to know Cignetti's assured, unapologetic style through his latest successes, at James Madison and then Indiana.

Love him or hate him, there's no doubting Cignetti's confidence — or his results. Both have defined his approach to the job far longer than you have known his name.

"I always felt," Cignetti said, "I'd be a good head coach."

CIGNETTI MAKES PEOPLE CARE ABOUT INDIANA FOOTBALL AGAIN

Cignetti's reputation has risen with his success. From transitioning James Madison from a Football Championship Subdivision power into a Sun Belt power to turning Indiana, a perennial cellar dweller, into a College Football Playoff team in 12 months, he has become one of the most recognizable faces — and quotes — in college football.

Depending largely upon your geographic persuasion, he has been a breath of fresh air invigorating a modern-day Big Ten success story or a try-hard coach from a try-hard conference taking shots at the SEC for attention.

Even that surely qualifies as remarkable. When was the last time Paul Finebaum cared so much about *Indiana?*

Cignetti's coaching story is as distinctive as his personality. He came to head coaching jobs late, and despite an impressive Power Four lineage, he went to the base of the pyramid before working his way up.

But he didn't appear out of thin air at Indiana University of Pennsylvania, anymore than he did Indiana University. Cignetti, 64, has known virtually his entire life he wanted this, and it's not much less time than that he has known he can do it this well.

"Probably third or fourth grade, when we went to West Virginia," Cignetti said, tracing his coaching ambition as far back as he could.

Frank Cignetti Sr. made that move with his family to Morgantown to join Bobby Bowden's staff ahead of the 1970

While college football fans were surprised by Indiana's early success under Curt Cignetti, his coaching track record prior to arriving in Bloomington was no fluke. RICH JANZARUK/HERALD-TIMES

season. Curt would watch from the sideline and occasionally sneak into the locker room.

The more he watched his father, the further in love with the sport Curt fell. He credits hard work for overcoming "average" athleticism, allowing him to play quarterback at West Virginia. But he always saw his future with a headset.

"With dad, you're living it," Curt Cignetti said. "As a competitive guy growing up, it really appealed to me."

CIGNETTI FOLLOWS HIS OWN BLUEPRINT FOR SUCCESS

That explains the why. Cignetti tweeted a picture of the how in the late hours of Dec. 18, 2023, just days after taking the Indiana job.

The tweet was captioned "Not done yet!" It featured a picture of Cignetti's desk in his new office overlooking the Memorial Stadium field, an office that's not altogether less spartan now than it was then.

Situated prominently was a book titled "James Madison Coaches Manual." It set off a tempest on James Madison Twitter, the suggestion being Cignetti had walked out the door with trade secrets.

But the manual — far from being JMU property — reflected a lifetime spent in coaching and a process refined across decades into what Cignetti now consistently refers to as his "blueprint" for success.

"He had it here. It was probably half of what it is now," said IUP coach Paul Tortorella, Cignetti's defensive coordinator and eventual successor. "We didn't stray from it."

Cignetti's teams evolved with the game.

When he left his assistant job with Nick Saban at Alabama after the 2010 season, the first teams Cignetti built at IUP rushed the ball roughly 2½ times more often than they passed it. In 2023, James Madison finished second in the Sun Belt in yards passing a game.

Cignetti never chained himself to a scheme. Just an attitude.

"His system works," said Jamree Kromah, a standout defensive end for Cignetti at James Madison now with the Chicago Bears. "He's a guy that's all about winning and competing, all at the same time."

What didn't change was Cignetti's approach — organization, discipline and clear-eyed focus on nothing but the task immediately at hand. All of it brewing a confidence that often preceded even on-field results.

By the time Cignetti's teams got to prove themselves in games, they already had proved themselves to themselves.

"He brought it Day 1," Elon coach Troy Trisciani said. "I remember our very first meeting, him talking to the staff and then to the team, about how it's all about our mindset. Playing fast, physical, relentless, and that there will be no self-imposed limitations."

Former Cignetti assistants and players will smile at the second part of that quote.

Trisciani, who followed Tortorella's path as Cignetti's defensive coordinator for two years at Elon before taking over for him as head coach, is repeating one of Cignetti's favorite phrases.

"We play every play one play at a time, six seconds a play. Every play's got a life of its own. Fast, physical, relentless. Smart, disciplined, poised. Not affected by success and failure. Never satisfied until the end of the game."

Spend more than a few minutes around Cignetti or ask him anything at all about his philosophy, and he's bound to repeat it, verbatim.

"There's even more of them," Tortorella said, "but that's one of the main ones."

Seeking meaning in mottos can be dangerous. But it surely reflects something fundamental in Cignetti that his mission statement has been so deeply ingrained into his working process that his coaches and players know it word for word.

And they see it in the way he works, the success he has and the things he leaves behind.

James Madison was the first of Cignetti's head jobs not to be handed off to one of his assistants. To this day, Tortorella said IUP still structured its practices and meetings with the same efficiency Cignetti always preached.

"Everything was today," Tortorella said. "Not yesterday, and not tomorrow. We do a lot of the same things now that we did when he was here."

He can be a tireless worker, often arriving to his office before sunup. On the morning of his first signing day with the Hoosiers, in December 2023, Cignetti was operating on so little rest he clipped a curb on his way into the team facility because he fell asleep at the wheel.

"My car dealer," he deadpanned, "is not going to be real happy with me."

But attend a Cignetti-led practice and you're bound to leave early. There is little wasted effort. And while he will keep both hands on the important tasks — Cignetti still manages Indiana's revenue-share payroll personally, for example — he knows when to delegate and what to leave alone.

All of it reflective of that process, one Cignetti turned into serious winning almost from the start.

Among the many elements that contribute to Curt Cignetti's winning ways, the consistency to his approach across all the teams that he has coached stands out. RICH JANZARUK/HERALD-TIMES

"He doesn't waste a lot of time," Tortorella said, "on things that really don't have anything to do with winning or losing."

RISKING FINANCIAL SECURITY BY BETTING ON HIS SKILL SET

But if you want him to pin it down, exactly when he knew that blueprint was laid out correctly, Cignetti will rewind to Alamance County in North Carolina.

Elon was, in Cignetti's words, "in worse shape from a competitive standpoint than Indiana" when he took the job. Yet behind freshman quarterback Davis Cheek, after losing Week 1 at Toledo, the Phoenix tore off a run of eight consecutive victories, none by more than one possession.

Eventually, that season ran aground with successive losses to three ranked teams. Furman eliminated Elon in the first round of the FCS playoffs. But Cignetti had manifested that confidence he had felt that day at his father's house. It validated his approach like nothing had previously.

"That first year at Elon, I felt like I kind of had it down," Cignetti said. "It just reinforced what I believe."

So has virtually everything since, up to and including Indiana's historic turnaround in the fall of 2024, from a 3-9 record to 11-2 and a CFP berth. But if that reinforced what Cignetti believes about his process, it did not necessarily convince a wider sport still doubting the Hoosiers today.

Cignetti came to head coaching late but supremely prepared. And an old backup quarterback knows nothing breeds confidence like preparation.

"You don't take that kind of chance that I took," Cignetti said, "leaving Alabama (to be) a DII head coach and dropped that kind of pay cut — with your kids, one in college, two in high school, wanting to be doctors — without believing in yourself."

Cignetti turned up at his father's that day in December 2016 so excited for the same reason he left Alabama for IUP.

The same reason he left James Madison for Indiana.

The same reason he had put a historical cellar dweller in the playoff conversation for the second year in a row.

He knows his process works. Hand him the chance, and Curt Cignetti will go out and kick some ass. ■

NO. 7 INDIANA 30, NO. 2 OREGON 20
OCTOBER 11, 2025 • EUGENE, OREGON

RESPONDING TO ADVERSITY

AFTER HIS PICK-SIX, MENDOZA DELIVERS SIX-MINUTE WINNING DRIVE

BY MICHAEL NIZIOLEK

Quarterback Fernando Mendoza orchestrated one of the most memorable drives in Indiana history during a 30-20 victory over second-ranked Oregon just moments after one of the lowest points in his career.

Mendoza threw a pick-six early in the fourth quarter that allowed the Ducks to score only their second touchdown to tie the top-10 showdown at 20. Mendoza was trying to avoid the sack, but he knew the moment the ball left his hand that he made a mistake.

It was a gut punch for the second-ranked Hoosiers, especially because Oregon's high-powered offense had been stuck in neutral.

Before Mendoza even got to the sideline, one by one, his teammates came up to him and offered words of encouragement. Linebacker Aiden Fisher was among the first.

"After the pick-six, Fish came up to me and said, 'Hey, brother, I have your back; I believe in you,'" Mendoza said. "And to have a team captain say that and come up to me, it inspires confidence, in not just me, (but) the entire offense."

To see his teammates united on the sideline put Mendoza's mind at ease, especially with the offense having to go right back onto the field against the favored Ducks (5-1, 2-1).

"That can be very frustrating for a defense that's played so well the entire game, for the offense to allow a touchdown," Mendoza said. "There was no panic. We knew we were going to have to overcome adversity at some point."

Indiana's offense still faced tense moments down the stretch — the Hoosiers had to convert on three third-down attempts and shrug off another in a long line of false starts — but Mendoza led them on a 12-play, 75-yard drive that lasted six minutes, 19 seconds. It ended with an 8-yard, back-shoulder throw to Elijah Sarratt.

It was a drive reminiscent of how Indiana (6-0, 3-0) operated for much of the season. Mendoza acted as a point guard and let his playmakers go to work. At one point, he set Sarratt up on a quick screen and the receiver burst up the sideline for 29 yards.

Mendoza's final line wasn't overly impressive. He was 20 of 31 for 215 yards passing with a touchdown and an interception, but he was right on target when the team needed him the most. He went 5 of 7 for 62 yards to put the Hoosiers back in front with 6:23 left in the game.

"We flushed it real quick," Sarratt said of the interception.

For Mendoza, the team's response proved what he knew in his heart about its character.

"We really banded together and became a stronger unit," he said. "I think that's what so special about Indiana football."

WITH A 58-YARDER, INDIANA'S SECONDARY KICKER TIES RECORD

Sixth-year place-kicker Brendan Franke might ask for two entries in the Indiana record book. His end-of-the-half, 58-yard field goal that handed the Hoosiers a 13-10 lead matched the IU record for longest field goal.

Griffin Oakes, a two-time Big Ten kicker of the year, set the record in 2014 at home against Maryland. But, thanks to Dan Lanning's icing time-out, Franke had to make the kick twice.

Field goals weren't Franke's stock and trade. A kickoff specialist who never played prep football and who never made a collegiate field goal, Franke was recruited out of Texas State to kick off this season. Before that, the former soccer goalie kicked off for Morningside, Nebraska and Georgia Southern. ■

Fernando Mendoza bounced back from a game-tying pick-six in the fourth quarter. On the decisive drive, he connected with Elijah Sarrat for 13 yards on a third-and-6 and for a touchdown on third-and-goal from the 8. BEN LONERGAN/EUGENE REGISTER-GUARD

INDIANA
15
9

IU FOOTBALL FINALLY HAS ITS GENERAL, AND CIGNETTI'S TEAM CAN BEAT ANYONE, ANYWHERE

BY GREGG DOYEL

Autzen Stadium is practically empty, except for one section near the end zone. That's where Indiana fans have gathered to celebrate the biggest victory in #iufb history — for now, anyway — this 30-20 smackdown of No. 2 Oregon, handing the Ducks their first loss in Big Ten play, ever, and snapping two Oregon winning streaks that had been, before the 2025 Indiana Hoosiers showed up, the longest such active streaks in college football:

- 18 consecutive home victories.
- 23 consecutive regular-season victories.

Done, done.

This was the No. 7 Hoosiers (6-0, 3-0 Big Ten) doing the almost unthinkable, going into Eugene, Oregon — into that sea of yellow-and-green — and playing offense with a silent count (so loud) and playing defense with a merciless mentality (so physical) and beating Oregon so thoroughly that Autzen Stadium was emptying well before IU quarterback Fernando Mendoza had lined up in the victory formation and knelt down once, twice, three times, four times.

But it wasn't completely empty. IU fans showed up, filling a handful of westbound planes and then filling a part of the stadium and then gathering near the end zone to thank the Hoosiers for the memory of a lifetime.

But here came the Hoosiers, thanking the fans, running to the front row — some of them jumping into the crowd or trying to get there. Defensive tackle Tyrique Tucker was jumping to get up there, but he's 6 feet, 302 pounds and tired from spending the previous 3½ hours in Oregon's backfield.

Now the rest of the traveling IU fan base — what, you thought it was just those fans near the end zone? — was heading toward the field, lining the front row, extending hands for the Hoosiers to slap as they took their victory lap around the most intimidating venue in college football. Indiana made itself at home at Autzen, kind of like Indiana made itself at home last year at the Rose Bowl in Pasadena, California, for the first Big Ten game of Curt Cignetti's tenure, that 42-13 blowout of UCLA.

But that crowd, in that venue, made sense. Pasadena had been settled in 1872 by a contingent of affluent families from Indianapolis. Oh, didn't you know? It's a true story.

Far as I know, the Hoosiers didn't settle Eugene. Sure looked comfortable there, though.

INDIANA FOOTBALL NOW CAN BEAT THE BIG BOYS

Oregon was too big, too fast. That's what people were thinking, and you couldn't blame them. Cignetti is brilliant at recruiting or game-planning or motivating or mining the transfer portal — or all of the above, most likely — but this IU team had limitations, same as last season. Not big enough. Not fast enough. Not to play with teams such as Ohio State and Notre Dame, who handed the Hoosiers their only losses last season ... by a combined score of 65-32. IU was skilled and smart, obviously, but not physically ready for Ohio State or Notre Dame then, or for Oregon now.

Turns out.

Once the biggest surprise in college football, Indiana has become something terrifying. Remember what happened last month when the Hoosiers played No. 8 Illinois? Destroyed the Illini 63-10. Only a powerhouse, a national championship contender, does something like that. Same with Saturday at Autzen: Only a national championship contender goes into that stadium and beats a team coached

Curt Cignetti shakes the hand of Oregon coach Dan Lanning before what would be one of two meetings during a memorable season for Indiana. BEN LONERGAN/EUGENE REGISTER-GUARD

by Dan Lanning — earlier this week Cignetti had called Lanning "one of the most impressive young coaching phenoms to come around in a while" — as emphatically as IU beat Oregon.

This was clear, from evidence statistical — IU outgained Oregon 326-267, including a 23-14 edge in first downs — and anecdotal.

Like, the time the pride of Lawrence North, IU receiver Omar Cooper Jr., made a leaping, one-handed grab and then shrugged off one tackler and dragged another tackler five yards before finally going down. Like, the time Cooper caught another short pass and was heading out of bounds but decided it would be more fun to lower his shoulder and ram into the nearest defensive back. Like, the time IU running back Roman Hemby scored the first of his two rushing touchdowns by exploding three yards into the end zone, pancaking Oregon's All-America safety, former Westfield and Purdue star Dillon Thieneman.

If the IU offense was hitting Oregon that hard, can you imagine what the IU defense was doing to the Ducks?

It looked like this: IU linebacker Rolijah Hardy grabbed running back Noah Whittington so hard around his clavicles, theatrically pulling Whittington around 180 degrees, that the crowd and CBS broadcast crew were convinced Hardy had grabbed Whittington's facemask. Nope. He just grabbed Whittington's jersey and jerked him to the ground.

And it looked like this: Oregon doing what it did under Lanning, going for it on fourth down whenever it felt like it, this time on the Ducks' first drive of the game, and Tucker chucking aside Oregon's center before making the stop for no gain on fourth-and-1 near midfield.

The Hoosiers made their intentions clear from the start. Oregon (5-1, 2-1) had allowed one sack all season. IU needed one play to record a sack, Mario Landino doing the honors to Oregon's Dante Moore on the first snap from scrimmage. The Hoosiers ended up with six sacks.

Indiana was hitting so hard, nobody was safe. On one Moore running play, IU linebacker Aiden Fisher and defensive lineman Mikail Kamara met Moore at the same time, from opposite directions, and the collision knocked Kamara woozy.

This whole thing was something Cignetti could see coming. No, not Fisher knocking Kamara out of the game for a play. This win. *That.*

"We had a great mindset coming in, and I really believed this could happen," he told CBS on the field afterward. "Had a couple great road wins the last three places I was at, and I just kind of felt this coming in."

MENDOZA: A TOP HEISMAN CANDIDATE, EVEN BETTER GUY

Not sure if this was the best moment of the game — not sure it wasn't — but it was the most typical Fernando Mendoza moment ever.

CBS is waiting to interview him on the field after the game, but there goes Mendoza, running toward the tunnel. Humble guy, Mendoza, the kind of fellow who thanks his God and his coaches and his teammates and even congratulates the other team for playing such a hard-fought game — after having a Heisman Trophy-like outing, as he did against Iowa — and now he's what, ducking national television to get to the locker room?

No. Better than that.

Mendoza is ducking national television to stop Oregon's quarterback from leaving the field too soon. Mendoza wants to tell Dante Moore: good game. Mendoza wants to wish him well going forward. Only then does Mendoza come back to the limelight, where he tells CBS — most typical Fernando Mendoza moment ever, I'm telling you — that he wants to thank God first, and then his family, and the offense, and the defense. Now he's singling out the receivers and running backs and offensive linemen, and applauding "a great team like Oregon."

Oh, and this:

"Thank you so much to Hoosier Nation for coming out," he says.

Hoosier Nation is getting the picture, loud and clear: This is a team worth watching, supporting, even following to the ends of the Big Ten and the contiguous United States; same thing, these days. And Hoosier Nation is falling more in love with Cignetti by the day, going on social media during this game to silence a typical Barstool Sports bully who'd taken a shot at Cignetti on X before kickoff, and even starting to compare him to — ready for this? — IU basketball legend Bob Knight.

It's true. All around social media, IU fans were seeing shades of "The General" in the way Cignetti stormed off the

Indiana players gather in the end zone to celebrate with a large contingent of crimson-clad fans. BEN LONERGAN/EUGENE REGISTER-GUARD

sideline, onto the field, into the face of multiple officials, when none of them called the blatant pass interference committed against receiver Elijah Sarratt. How do you know it was blatant pass interference? Because Sarratt, who had eight catches for 121 yards and a touchdown, didn't catch that one. More to the point: The receiver they call "Waffle House" — Sarratt's always open, get it? — wasn't open. Clearly someone cheated, and officials missed it, and Cignetti went *off*.

"Can't let that go," Cignetti told CBS at halftime.

That interview came moments after one of the more ice-veinous things you'll ever see: Brendan Franke, the Hoosiers' kickoff specialist, drilling a 58-yard field goal with one second on the clock ... only to have it nullified by a late time-out called by Lanning. So, Franke does it again, kicking another 58-yarder — would've been good from 65 — to tie the school record.

The Hoosiers went into halftime leading 13-10 and dominated the Ducks the rest of the way, the final score being as close as it was only because we finally saw proof that Mendoza wasn't perfect. He threw a pass off his back foot, didn't get enough on it and watched helplessly as Brandon Finney Jr. intercepted it and returned it 35 yards for a touchdown that tied the game at 20.

From there the Hoosiers asserted their dominance — against Oregon, at Oregon, think about that — and were kneeling in the final minute or could have scored again. But the job was already done. Big Ten newbie Oregon, 11-0 all-time in league play, had finally lost one. The Hoosiers, 0-46 all-time on the road against top-5 competition, had finally won one.

Their first one, that is. ■

ON THE SAME PAGE

IN A JIFFY, INDIANA INKS CIGNETTI TO A $93 MILLION EXTENSION

BY ZACH OSTERMAN AND MICHAEL NIZIOLEK | OCTOBER 16, 2025

So quickly did Curt Cignetti's new, improved eight-year Indiana contract come together, it was announced via tweet. Well, tweets. First, one confirming the deal, accompanied by a picture of Cignetti at his desk in his office, signing a piece of paper. His preferred Glacier Freeze Gatorade Zero sat to one side.

The second tweet contained a 46-second message accompanying the news. Somewhere between signing and speaking, Cignetti must have taken a sip, because he didn't bother to put the cap back on.

He had more important things to worry about.

"We've accomplished a lot here in a short amount of time," Cignetti told the camera, "but still have a lot of work to do. I couldn't be more proud to be a Hoosier, and I plan on retiring as a Hoosier.

"The way that this state has embraced us and our success in football has meant more to me than anything else. So, I just wanted to get on camera and let you know that Curt Cignetti is gonna work daily to make Indiana the best it can be."

If there comes a time when we're required to pinpoint the exact moment Indiana pivoted firmly to football, this might be it.

In the days that followed the announcement of Cignetti's third contract with Indiana in less than two years, the coach revealed how the negotiations went down and the university revealed the details of the deal.

Cignetti told reporters that on the Tuesday following the 30-20 victory over Oregon — the second victory over a top-5 opponent in IU history — athletic director Scott Dolson dropped by his office earlier than their weekly meeting. He proposed a new contract because of the series of high-profile jobs opening up across the country.

Two days earlier, Penn State fired James Franklin after 12 seasons and a .698 winning percentage. Before the season's halfway point, Arkansas, Oklahoma State, UCLA and Virginia Tech already had jettisoned their coaches. Power Four coaches were on hot seats across the nation, including those at Florida, Florida State, Auburn, Kentucky and Michigan State.

"He popped in for about a minute and a half said, 'This is kind of what we'd like to do. OK if we call your representative?'" Cignetti said. "I said, 'Sure, it would be great.' Within 48 hours, 36 hours, it was done."

The new contract called for Cignetti to make $93 million over eight years. For 2025-26, his pay was bumped from $8.3 million to $11.15 million. That moved him from the country's 18th-highest paid coach to the fifth, according to USA TODAY Sports' coaching salary database.

Ahead of Cignetti were Georgia's Kirby Smart ($13.3 million), Ohio State's Ryan Day ($12.6 million), USC's Lincoln Riley ($11.5 million) and Clemson's Dabo Swinney ($11.4 million). All but Riley had won national championships.

Cignetti's deal featured a base salary of $500,000, an annual retention bonus of $1 million (which increased to $1.25 million in 2029) and annual outside marketing and promotional income starting at $9.65 million (which topped out at $10.35 million).

In 2032-33 — when he would be 72 years old — Cignetti's total compensation would be $12.1 million. ■

With big-time jobs open and more on the horizon, Indiana tried to prevent desperate athletic directors from pursuing Curt Cignetti by making him the country's fifth-highest paid coach as part of an eight-year contract. CHRIS PIETSCH/EUGENE REGISTER-GUARD

NO. 3 INDIANA 38, MICHIGAN STATE 13
OCTOBER 18, 2025 · BLOOMINGTON, INDIANA

NO MORE MR. NICE GUY

CIGNETTI LAYS DOWN THE LAW AFTER SLOPPY PRACTICE

BY MICHAEL NIZIOLEK

Coach Curt Cignetti told reporters after Indiana's 38-13 victory over Michigan State that he had to be the bad guy during the week to get his team focused for the game.

The message he delivered at the start of the week about ripping off the rearview mirror didn't land the way it needed to coming off the historic victory at Oregon.

After what multiple players admitted was a sloppy Thursday practice, Cignetti gathered the No. 3 Hoosiers (7-0, 4-0 Big Ten) to make certain they understood he wasn't pleased by their lack of focus.

"Look, you can't be a real nice guy when you have a job like mine, you know what I mean?" Cignetti said. "Sometimes you know when they're going to be ready to play and then sometimes you know the entire organization —what did Mike Krzyzewski say when he retired? He said the toughest opponent he's ever faced was human nature."

Cignetti knew in this case that meant feeling "happy and relaxed" after picking up the kind of signature victory historically hard to come by for the Hoosiers. They went to Oregon with a 1-72 all-time record against top-5 opponents.

They came out of the weekend with the No. 3 ranking in both national polls — the highest in IU history — but none of that was going to matter against Michigan State.

Receiver Elijah Sarratt, with Cignetti going back to the 2023 season at James Madison, had seen the coach take that kind of hardline approach in the past. One of the more recent examples came on the Friday before IU's game against Kennesaw State: Cignetti ripped into the team after a lackadaisical walk-through.

"Y'all ain't seen him like that," Sarratt said. "It gets gritty in there when he gets in that mode, but usually it's good for us."

The message usually landed because that wasn't necessarily Cignetti's default approach.

Quarterback Fernando Mendoza credited Cignetti's daily pep talks for helping the Hoosiers build up the "indomitable will" they needed to beat a talented team like Oregon on the road. Cignetti centered those team meetings on how to handle adversity.

He inspired the urgency his team needed this week by changing up the delivery.

"Coach Cignetti after practice gave a great talk ... about not being complacent," Mendoza said. "That Michigan State is a great team, it's a rivalry game and anything can happen. We got to really attack this game as hard and with the effort and focus to become victorious over Oregon."

Well, the Old Brass Spittoon will reside in Bloomington for at least two more years. The teams don't meet again until 2027, and the Hoosiers have won the last two meetings, their first back-to-back victories in the series since three straight in 1967-69.

The IU offense scored on its first five possessions, which led to a 35-10 advantage late in the third quarter. However, the defense struggled to find its footing against MSU and quarterback Aidan Chiles and twice trailed in the first half.

MSU (3-4, 0-4) used 6:53 on the opening possession to drive 55 yards in 13 plays for a 38-yard field goal. Indiana responded with a 15-play drive that ended with a 13-yard touchdown pass from Mendoza to E.J. Williams Jr.

But the Spartans answered with a 12-play, 75-yard drive that lasted 8:18, ended in a TD and produced a 10-7 lead.

The Hoosiers scored 31 straight points with Mendoza on cruise control as the student section chanted "HeisMendoza." He threw scoring strikes to Elijah Sarratt (24 and 27 yards) and to Omar Cooper Jr. (48 yards) en route to 332

Indiana wide receiver E.J. Williams Jr. dives for a 13-yard touchdown in the first quarter despite a trio of Spartans intent on stopping him. Quarterback Fernando Mendoza threw as many TD passes (four) as incompletions (24-for-28). RICH JANZARUK/HERALD-TIMES

yards. He threw as many TDs (four) as he did incompletions (24-for-28).

"I did hear on the field," Mendoza said. "I want to give a shout-out to the student section for sticking through the rain and the shirtless towel-waving. That was fantastic to see them. All the players on the sideline were hyped about it. It got myself juiced, the offense juiced, the team juiced."

Fans had to clear the stadium during halftime because of lightning in the area. The student section was fired up when allowed back and stayed engaged through the rain until the final buzzer.

"What a great sight to see," Mendoza said.

He was tight-lipped about his Heisman Trophy candidacy, continuing a trend.

"Whatever spotlight that I might get from the offense's success," he said, "I'm trying to dish it all out to my teammates. They really deserve it."

In the end, the Hoosiers paraded the Old Brass Spittoon around Memorial Stadium. And Cignetti even cracked a smile or two during his postgame news conference.

"My job is to make sure they've got the right mindset ready to play," he said. "It's not always fun, but you've got to do what you've got to do." ■

NO. 2 INDIANA 56, UCLA 6
OCTOBER 25, 2025 • BLOOMINGTON, INDIANA

GETTING NASTY

RELENTLESS DEFENSIVE LINE LEAVES BRUINS IN RUINS

BY MICHAEL NIZIOLEK

After a 56-6 loss to Indiana, UCLA interim coach Tim Skipper said his team never recovered from throwing a pick-six to linebacker Aiden Fisher on the second play of the game.

It probably didn't help that quarterback Nico Iamaleava was sacked by defensive tackle Tyrique Tucker and linebacker Rolijah Hardy on the first play.

Skipper said his offense was "shellshocked" when the Bruins got the ball back and played like it.

"We didn't really bounce back from that moment," he said.

The constant pressure from Indiana's defensive line was a big reason why. The D-line combined for 23 quarterback pressures, five tackles for loss and 1½ sacks. Six of the eight linemen came up with at least one quarterback pressure.

"We did not win in the trenches," Skipper said. "We did not move them."

The Hoosiers (8-0, 5-0 Big Ten) moved up to second in the polls after the Michigan State game because No. 2 Miami (Florida) lost to Louisville 24-21. Ohio State remained atop the US LBM Coaches Poll with all 65 first-place votes, which meant pollster Curt Cignetti voted for the Buckeyes.

UCLA fired coach DeShaun Foster after three losses to open his second season. Right after, defensive coordinator Ikaika Malloe got the boot. After a 17-14 loss at Northwestern in Week 4, the ax fell on offensive coordinator Tino Sunseri, who left his job as IU's quarterbacks coach to head out West.

Victories followed over Penn State, Michigan State and Maryland, which promoted Cignetti say the Bruins were playing as well as any team in the country.

"We're playing a 3-0 football team that's undefeated, 3-0 in the conference," he said. "Since they have retooled their staff, now have their new defensive coordinator and offensive staff in place, very impressive football team, OK?"

Not so much after 51 seconds in Bloomington.

On the opening play, Tucker offered a glimpse at how the rest of the game would unfold. He shoved guard Yutaka Mahe to the side and tied up Iamaleava as Hardy and three other Hoosiers swarmed to the ball.

On second-and-12, the Bruins (3-5, 3-2) tried to chip edge rusher Stephen Daley with a tight end only for it to end in disaster. Daley, a Kent State transfer who was making his first IU start in place of injured Kellan Wyatt, finished the game with seven pressures to give him 16 over the last two games.

Fisher picked off Iamaleava at the UCLA 25 and dashed to the end zone.

Tucker traced the D-line's inspired effort to a challenge from the coaching staff after a less than stellar game against Michigan State. Defensive coordinator Bryant Haines shared a similar critique following the opener against Old Dominion.

"We didn't play aggressive enough," Tucker said. "This week he had to go show them."

According to Skipper, UCLA also struggled with Haines' scheme from the stunts and twists he liked to call up front to the simulated pressures. One glaring example came late in the first quarter with the Bruins trying to convert a third-and-8.

Indiana appeared to be rushing six defenders with the two linebackers on the field, Hardy and Isaiah Jones, showing a blitz. Tackle Mario Landino executed a twist with Hardy while end Mikail Kamara dropped back in coverage.

Hardy and Jones teamed up for the sack, but Landino and Daley could have easily brought Iamaleava down as well.

Tucker picked up his second sack on a stunt with the Bruins facing a third-and-6 midway through the second quarter. UCLA left tackle Courtland Ford wasn't initially sure who to pick up when Daley bounced to the inside, and

A sixth-year defensive lineman at his third school, Dominique Ratcliff puts the clamps on UCLA's Nico Iamaleava.
RICH JANZARUK/HERALD-TIMES

Tucker took advantage of that indecisiveness.

"They're nasty up front, they play hard and aggressive," Jones said, "and with the stunts we have, those guys, it will free them up and they will be able to make plays."

KEEPING HEISMAN HYPE 'INSIDE THE BUILDING'

On Indiana's first drive, Fernando Mendoza threw an interception on a pass batted at the line of scrimmage. He almost had as many incompletions on that drive (three) as he did in the entire game against the Spartans (four), and the passing game remained stuck in neutral for most of the afternoon.

It didn't matter. Mendoza still threw three TD passes and scored on a 20-yard run.

He continued to avoid Heisman hype as much as possible. He texted during the week with former Heisman winner Matt Leinart for advice, and Mendoza said his strategy would be to keep everything "inside the building."

"Today, was a great win, but I still started the game out a little sloppy and wasn't great on my technique," Mendoza said. "I don't want to listen to the outside noise and hear 'that's so great' and then forget about those issues I need to build on."

He had long-since deleted nearly all social media accounts off his phone outside of LinkedIn and YouTube. He had an active Instagram account run by his brother Alberto and his marketing people, and his YouTube habits feed back into his focus on football.

"I usually watch NFL highlights," Mendoza said with laugh. "Sometimes Kurt Warner breakdowns." ■

Before the UCLA game, Indiana fans turn out in droves for Fox's "Big Noon Kickoff" pregame show on campus. RICH JANZARUK/HERALD-TIMES

BIG NOON KICKOFF

UNIVERSITY
FOX BIG NOON KICKOFF
INDIANA
HOW 'CIG STOLE THE B1G
Ucla BRUINS
HOOSIER DADDY?
GO IU!!!
COOKIES OR BROWNIES?
HOOSIER DADDY
EVEN TERRY
SMOKIN A PACK OF BRUINS
GO HOOSIERS
SATURDAY

NO. 2 INDIANA 55, MARYLAND 10
NOVEMBER 1, 2025 · COLLEGE PARK, MARYLAND

UNSTOPPABLE

IT WILL TAKE SOMETHING REMARKABLE TO DERAIL IU JUGGERNAUT

BY ZACH OSTERMAN

Word got around College Park, late in the week, that Maryland finally sold out its homecoming game. It came as a minor surprise. Good tickets remained available as recently as Monday. Mike Locksley's Terrapins were in the midst of another mid-season slump, a common feature of his tenure, and yet, by Saturday morning, all seats were accounted for, if not necessarily filled at kickoff.

The answer to that late-breaking demand stared back from the sections of SECU Stadium that filled in by the start of the game. The alumni base recently declared America's largest — with healthy representation in major metropolitan areas up and down the Atlantic Seaboard — arrived in force. From D.C., New York and Philadelphia, Indiana fans made their presence felt in yet another road environment turned because of the score and the visiting crowd into friendly confines by game's end.

The several thousand fans wearing Indiana crimson who stayed through all four quarters of a 55-10 blowout roared as Curt Cignetti led his Hoosiers off the field. They cheered for a team they had come to love, one so deeply motivated by its ambitions and so completely in tune with Cignetti's relentless fight for focus that seemingly nothing could break its stride.

"Every single week," edge rusher Mikail Kamara said, "we've got to make sure there's no doubt left, at all."

There could be none remaining, as second-ranked Indiana (9-0, 6-0) strode off into the cool Maryland night having bulldozed its way through another blowout.

The nation's leader in margin of victory heading into the weekend only improved on that number emerging out of it. This time the methods were different, because the opponent was different and so the challenge was different.

But the result was the same. The Hoosiers had won their nine games by an average of 35.7 points.

Fernando Mendoza (14 of 21 passing, 225 total yards, two touchdowns) started slowly and so did his offense. An interception ended IU's first drive and a sack doomed the second.

So, Bryant Haines' defense went to work on Malik Washington, the promising but inexperienced freshman Maryland (4-4, 1-4) lines up behind center. Washington had played beyond his years at times this season, helped by offensive coordinator Pep Hamilton's ability to simplify and smooth for his young quarterback.

Hamilton could do nothing for Washington this day, other than a reassuring arm around the shoulder afterward and the promise that most days weren't this hard.

Because most defenses weren't this good. Indiana allowed just 293 yards, a healthy chunk of those gained long after the result was beyond doubt.

The Hoosiers flipped their script — finishing with no sacks and just three tackles for loss; instead, they turned Maryland over five times.

That's as many turnovers as Locksley's team had committed all season before Saturday.

"The defense has, all year long, risen to the occasion when their backs are against the wall," Cignetti said. "It wasn't perfect tonight defensively, trust me. ... But there's a lot of good things there on tape."

OK, so maybe it wouldn't be Washington's arm, or Mendoza's slow start, or the turnover differential that untracked the freight train this team had become.

Maybe injuries would do the trick.

Linebacker Aiden Fisher, who Cignetti described as probable Monday, drifted toward questionable as the week

Fired up after a second-quarter touchdown pass, Fernando Mendoza let out a yell before celebrating with his teammates. The pass covered 22 yards to Omar Cooper Jr. In the first quarter, Mendoza scored on a 7-yard run. TOMMY GILLIGAN/IMAGN IMAGES

wore on. He watched from the sideline. Drew Evans was a surprise absence, with Cignetti suggesting his starting left guard could miss several weeks.

In the game itself, IU lost wide receiver Elijah Sarratt (hamstring) and linebacker Kaiden Turn (calf) and helped offensive lineman Kahlil Benson (ankle/foot) play his way through pain until his efforts were no longer required.

Surely, between a starting lineman, a linebacker captain and the Hoosiers' leading receiver, the sheer weight of injuries would affect this team's performance. Not a chance.

"It's just the trust we have in each other," Mendoza said. "We know we have each other's backs, and it's one group going toward one goal."

Maryland, Mendoza said, responded to Sarratt's departure by committing to coverage and refusing to lose the game in the air. Indiana just made the Terrapins lose it on the ground.

IU's 367 yards rushing were the most in a game since the fan-favorite Bacon And Legs victory over Maryland in 2016. Three backs ran for at least 80 yards, and four Hoosiers (including Mendoza) rushed for a touchdown.

Backup (and little brother) Alberto Mendoza's 53-yard run in the fourth quarter, the Hoosiers' longest of the day, tacked one final flourish onto a signature afternoon. Everyone contributed to another remarkable performance, and so everyone shared at least a little bit of the credit.

There's every chance, though, that IU sees some of those important absent faces back on the field in a week in State College. And there's just as much chance it won't matter either way.

The relentlessness with which his team wins games is what puts all the sport's biggest prizes in front of this team. At some point, we might find an opponent or an obstacle that could break Indiana's unrelenting forward progress, but it's going to take something remarkable to do it. ■

NO. 2 INDIANA 27, PENN STATE 24
NOVEMBER 8, 2025 • STATE COLLEGE, PENNSYLVANIA

DON'T WORRY, BE HAPPY

INCREDIBLE THROW, IMPOSSIBLE CATCH PRESERVE PERFECT SEASON

BY GREGG DOYEL

On the play of the season for Indiana football — the play of this season, last season, any season — IU quarterback Fernando Mendoza makes an impossible throw and IU receiver Omar Cooper Jr. makes an impossible catch.

Mendoza hasn't been having a great day Saturday for the Hoosiers at Penn State, but in 71 seconds he has driven the second-ranked Hoosiers from their 20 to the Penn State 7. Happy Valley is furious and Beaver Stadium is thundering and it's third-and-goal from the Nittany Lions' 7 with 40 seconds left. Mendoza drops back, and this is how it has been all game: He's about to get hit. Sometimes the pressure has been in his face. Sometimes it's come from his blindside.

Well, here it's both.

Mendoza is in the pocket, about to be sandwiched between two blitzing Nittany Lions, when he throws a pass toward the back of the end zone. Toward Cooper.

Cooper hasn't been having a great day, but he caught a 22-yard pass earlier in this drive and now he's running along the back of the end zone, watching the football come his way, and this one won't be easy. The ball is sailing — on the television set, Fox analyst Joel Klatt muses that Mendoza was trying to throw the ball away — but Cooper is tracking it and he's a former basketball star and high jumper at Lawrence North, so you know he can jump. He's leaping and grabbing the football, which isn't easy, but here comes the hard part:

The Penn State defender, Zakee Wheatley, is shoving Cooper over the back line of the end zone. Cooper is helpless up there, way up there, in midair as his body starts heading out of bounds. Well, this was only third down. There's always fourth dow—

Wait, what did he just do?

Cooper's upper body is hovering above and beyond the out of bounds line, but he's stretching back his right foot. Stretching, stretching, stretching. He's descending. His right foot is stretching. Maybe it grazes the grass in bounds, maybe it doesn't, but get this:

Now he's stretching back his *left* foot. Stretching, stretching, stretching. He's still descending — the guy can really jump — and his left foot is still stretching, and it absolutely pokes the grass in the end zone.

Which foot was in bounds, his left or his right? It doesn't matter. One of them did, maybe both, before any part of his body touched out of bounds.

Mendoza's impossible pass – ever tried to throw a ball from the inside of a Nittany Lion *sandwich?* – and Cooper's impossible catch have given the Hoosiers a 27-24 victory, maintaining their perfect record, resume and argument as the best team of the 2025 college football season.

This was a victory that all but guaranteed the Hoosiers a first-round bye in the College Football Playoff, meaning they should advance directly to the quarterfinals with the other top four seeds, regardless of what happens Dec. 6 in the Big Ten championship game at Lucas Oil Stadium. Who knows, IU might beat No. 1 Ohio State that night in downtown Indianapolis. Might not. Either way, the Hoosiers will surely — right? — be a top-four seed going into the playoffs.

That pass from Mendoza did it. And that catch from Cooper did it.

Well, here it's both.

Fernando Mendoza keeps the Hoosiers unbeaten with big throws during a 10-play, 80-yard drive in the last two minutes. He scored the game's first touchdown on an 18-yard run. MATTHEW O'HAREN/IMAGN IMAGES

B1G
HOOSIERS
15

FOR A CHANGE, CIGNETTI DROPS HIS GAME FACE

Did his voice crack? Curt Cignetti sure seemed to be on the verge of something emotional — looked it a little and sounded it a lot — during his postgame interview there on the field with Fox's Jenny Taft. Earlier in the interview he had been calm, explaining this remarkable victory like so:

"Refuse to lose, basically," he said.

Only now Taft is asking him to expound on the Hoosiers' comeback on the road, their final drive, that game-winning touchdown. Cignetti is thinking about all of it, and no doubt thinking about the coincidence, the timing — this game happening in the state where his dad, Frank, was a college coaching legend, and where Curt Cignetti himself was born, raised and got his start in coaching — when he comes up with this answer:

"I've seen a lot of stuff in my day," he says, his voice starting to quiver. "I've never seen anything quite like this."

Now the interview is over, and Cignetti is walking away. This is a perfectionist, somebody who never-never-ever seems satisfied, but maybe this is different. Maybe this, finally, is what perfect looks like.

Because Cignetti is walking away from the interview, toward the locker room, toward his team — and he lets out a primal scream.

CHARLIE WHO? BECKER DELIVERS CLUTCH CATCHES

IU football was legit before this game, and in a vacuum, beating this particular Penn State team doesn't mean a whole lot. The Nittany Lions began the season with the same ranking the Indiana Hoosiers have now — No. 2 in the country — but along the way Penn State has lost quarterback Drew Allar (injured Oct. 11), coach James Franklin (fired the next day), and five consecutive games (all in the Big Ten).

This season, everyone who's anyone is beating the Nittany Lions (3-6, 0-6), but this game was different. Namely, this was the game where Indiana (10-0, 7-0) proved it had more than the starting lineup of a national contender. This was the game where the Hoosiers confirmed they had elite depth as well.

Indiana played the game without its most prolific TD-scoring receiver, Elijah Sarratt (hamstring), and played most of it without two of their five starting offensive linemen (left guard Drew Evans, right tackle Kahlil Benson). Its depth along the defensive line also was tested, but the Hoosiers had enough to finish this game.

The star of the day, in the macro sense — Mendoza and Cooper get the micro honors — was sophomore receiver Charlie Becker, who came into the game with seven catches in 21 career games but had seven catches on Saturday, each more ridiculous than the last. And one of his first catches was a 53-yarder that led to Mendoza's 18-yard scoring scramble late in the first quarter.

But after that came a leaping 10-yard catch in tight coverage, then a 13-yard reception where he was absolutely crushed as the ball touched his hands, and finally the 17-yarder that put the Hoosiers at the Penn State 7, setting up Mendoza-to-Cooper for the game-winner. On the 17-yard catch, Becker ran a sideline fade route and won a jump ball against a Penn State defensive back, landing on his back out of bounds – but not before he'd tapped his left foot in bounds.

Foreshadowing, you call that.

Because two plays later, after the Penn State defensive line made a mess of two consecutive passes by Mendoza — tipping one at the line of scrimmage, then forcing another incompletion by sending an untouched blitzer into his face — Mendoza drops back and Cooper is running along the back of the end zone and you know what happens next.

Indiana wins a 10th consecutive game, for the second consecutive season, to set up a pair of imminently winnable games — against Wisconsin (2-6) and at Purdue (2-8) — before the Big Ten title game. Perfection remains possible. Mendoza-to-Cooper made sure of that.

Indiana is No. 2 in the country and barreling toward a showdown with No. 1 Ohio State, then a legitimate shot at the national title. Forgive IU football fans if they're getting emotional, but they've seen a lot of stuff in their day — they've never seen anything quite like this. ■

After the Nittany Lions scored 17 straight points, Indiana quieted Penn State's student section with a spirited fourth-quarter comeback.
MATTHEW O'HAREN/IMAGN IMAGES

PENN STATE
NITTANY LIONS
PENN STATE
PENNSTATE
PENN STATE
PENNSTATE
24

A REAL TOE-TAPPER

HOW COOPER COMPLETED THE CATCH OF THE SEASON

BY MICHAEL NIZIOLEK

The Toe-tap.

Tappy Valley.

The 10-0 Tiptoe.

Whatever the name, Omar Cooper Jr.'s go-ahead touchdown catch in the 27-24 victory over Penn State will be a moment that will be talked about by Indiana fans for generations to come.

Cooper, a former Lawrence North star, made a leaping grab at the back of the end zone with 36 seconds to go that helped the second-ranked Hoosiers (10-0, 7-0 Big Ten) match their best start in program history. Cooper, a 6-foot redshirt junior wide receiver, managed to get his left foot down in bounds despite safety Zakee Wheatley pushing him out of the back of the end zone.

"I knew where I was in the field," Cooper said. "When I went up for the ball, I was just trying to get my feet as far inside as I could and make sure I came down with it."

In the nosebleed seats at Beaver Stadium, the pair of fans decked out in Omar Cooper Jr. gear celebrated the score before the officials finished reviewing the play.

"I saw his focus," said Cooper's mother, Vnemina. "He didn't just get one toe down, he got two."

The nerves they felt while watching Indiana give up a double-digit lead in the fourth quarter gave way to joy as Cooper's teammates mobbed him in the end zone.

"It was a rush of adrenaline, a rush of happiness," Omar Sr. said.

The smiles never left their faces when they relived the moment together outside the stadium. Omar Jr.'s parents were among the fans that gave IU players a sendoff near the team buses.

They got a chance to briefly chat with their son about the history-making catch before he headed back to Bloomington.

"You are just so thankful," Vnemina said. "You see the hard work he put in as a child all the way to IU. To know he has the determination to help the team anyway he can, it just makes my heart so proud."

Despite being targeted by Fernando Mendoza nine times and making six catches, Cooper had a relatively quiet afternoon until the game-winning drive. He finished with 32 yards, most coming on one play.

Mendoza didn't look Cooper's way in the first quarter. His three catches in the second quarter produced minus-four, zero and seven yards. His catch in the third quarter went for no goal.

Indiana's decisive drive started at its 20 with 1:51 left. On the first play, Mendoza was sacked. On second-and-17, he hit Cooper at the IU 32, and Cooper reached the 35 for a 22-yard gain.

Two plays later, from near midfield, Mendoza and Cooper couldn't connect on a deep ball. Eventually facing third-and-goal for the PSU 7, Mendoza zinged the ball over the defender, Cooper skied for it and his left foot did the rest.

Although his parents had never seen their son make a catch as meaningful as this one, the athletic ability and body control he displayed were familiar.

It harkened back to Omar Jr.'s days on the hardwood as a decorated basketball player and high jumper. He displayed a leaping ability well beyond his years and was known for throwing down the occasional windmill slam.

"We definitely weren't shocked he could get that high," Omar Sr. said.

The Coopers decorated their basement with photos of those moments, and the toe-tap likely will garner a prominent place on their walls soon.

"To keep that toe in bounds," coach Curt Cignetti said, "you gotta be a real special player to do that."

As a Nittany Lion tries to shove him out of the back of the the end zone, Omar Cooper Jr. secures the football and manages to land his left foot inside the boundary. The 7-yard touchdown put Indiana up 27-24 with 36 seconds left. MATTHEW O'HAREN/IMAGN IMAGES

HOOSIERS

NO. 2 INDIANA 31, WISCONSIN 7
NOVEMBER 15, 2025 • BLOOMINGTON, INDIANA

HOME COOKING

HOOSIERS TAKE OWNERSHIP OF NATION'S LONGEST HOME WINNING STREAK

BY MICHAEL NIZIOLEK AND ZACH OSTERMAN

Indiana football has come a long way from Curt Cignetti sending emails encouraging fans to pack Memorial Stadium and stay until the clock hit zero.

The second-ranked Hoosiers (11-0, 8-0) wrapped up a second straight undefeated season at home with a 31-7 victory over Wisconsin. When No. 4 Alabama fell to No. 10 Oklahoma 23-21 at Tuscaloosa several hours later, Indiana owned the longest active home winning streak at 15 games. The Crimson Tide had won 17 straight at Bryant-Denny Stadium.

Cignetti didn't need to prod the fan base this season — IU sold out its entire Big Ten schedule — and the 55,042 fans Saturday remained in their seats the entire way.

"We feed off of their energy," Cignetti said. "I really think that us playing at home is at least a 14-point advantage."

Cignetti's comments might seem like hyperbole, but the numbers back him up.

The Hoosiers have beaten their opponents by an average of 37.9 points at Memorial Stadium during his second-year tenure. In 2025, they won by an average of 40.7 points and didn't play a single game decided by single digits.

They beat three teams by 50 or more points, and two victories were against Big Ten opponents — Illinois when ranked eighth and UCLA when riding a three-game winning streak.

"Our fans are the best in America," Cignetti said. "I know where we started and where we are now, and they are over the top. I can't say enough good things about them."

Indiana has sold out 18 games since the stadium expanded in 1970 to hold 50,000-plus, and eight of those sellouts occurred during Cignetti's tenure.

"We don't know for a fact that it is our last game here at home," he said. "We hope it is. It's kind of weird to say."

The Hoosiers end the regular season with a bye week — once seemingly oddly timed but now fortuitous because of fatigue and injuries — and the 100th battle for the Old Oaken Bucket. A victory would ensure IU's first berth in the Big Ten championship game and quite likely a top-four finish in the final College Football Playoff rankings. That would include a bye into the quarterfinals — and mean Memorial Stadium had hosted its last game until Sept. 5, when the Mean Green of North Texas would open the 2026 season.

Against the Badgers (3-7, 1-6), despite what Cignetti acknowledged as a "lethargic" start, the Hoosiers moved to 11-0 for the first time in its history. Fernando Mendoza threw for 299 yards and four touchdowns, including a 5-yarder in the fourth quarter that broke Kurtis Rourke's single-season (and one-year-old) record of 29 TDs.

Indiana wasn't really in trouble despite only leading 10-7 at the half. Even after Wisconsin tied the game with a clever fourth-down call in the second quarter, the Hoosiers' win probability, per ESPN, never dipped lower than 93%.

Still, Mendoza was sacked five times. Indiana rushed for only 83 yards. Injuries mounted on the lines, and Elijah Sarratt (hamstring) missed his second straight game.

But Mendoza turned in his best game since homecoming against Michigan State on Oct. 18. He was back to his pitch-and-catch best, sprinkling in a few truly excellent throws into a 22 of 24 performance. Two third-quarter TD passes — a 2-yarder to Holden Staes and a 21-yarder to Riley Nowakowski — snuffed out any chance of an upset. In that quarter, IU outgained Wisconsin 135 yards to 11. ■

Tight end Riley Nowakowski evades two Badgers en route to a 21-yard touchdown reception that put Indiana ahead 24-7 in the third quarter. It was Fernando Mendoza's 29th TD toss of the season, tying the IU record Kurtis Rourke set in 2024. RICH JANZARUK/HERALD-TIMES

YOU

NO. 2 INDIANA 56, PURDUE 3
NOVEMBER 28, 2025 • WEST LAFAYETTE, INDIANA

'LET'S HAVE MORE FUN'

IU FINISHES FIRST PERFECT SEASON WITH ANOTHER BUCKET BLOWOUT

BY ZACH OSTERMAN

Speaking in the afterglow of his team's senior day victory over Wisconsin almost two weeks ago, Curt Cignetti admitted he struggled in the moment for perspective.

That a man in his position finds it difficult to "step back" — his words — "and think about what we've accomplished here" is understandable. Yet that perspective came easier Friday night, as Indiana clinched its first appearance in the Big Ten championship game with a 56-3 destruction of Purdue at Ross-Ade Stadium, which was painted crimson by the very success Cignetti can't allow himself to soak in for fear of the complacency it might feed.

In that same monologue earlier this month, Cignetti allowed for himself the best advice he could give his fans. Words that frame perfectly these heady, historic days for the program Cignetti has turned into the national force he said he would.

"It's been fun," Cignetti said. "Let's have more fun."

For Indiana football, these are the glory days. They may yet last awhile. None endure forever. Best enjoy these while they do.

Each week brings another first since, or never before, this season a race to rewrite as much of the record book as possible. Last season was the whirlwind rise, the season when nothing could go wrong because too much had gone right. It included a 66-0 victory over Purdue. But this season will be remembered forever.

The hows and whys of Friday night won't matter to anyone not of an Indiana persuasion. Fans get another year to bathe in a dominant rivalry showing, and this was certainly that. But on the field, the second-ranked Hoosiers are chasing something far greater than an Old Oaken Bucket.

Whatever happens across the next eight days, or the next six weeks, this season has changed so much about Indiana for the foreseeable future. Maybe for good.

And while Cignetti and his players have the big prizes firmly in their sights, there should be nothing wrong with stopping for a moment to appreciate that seasons like these will in their own way last forever.

"First team in Indiana history to go 12-0 in the regular season," Cignetti said. "That's absolute. Whatever happens from here, this team will always be the first team."

On the topic of those hows and whys, Cignetti will have enjoyed them Friday.

He said he felt the Hoosiers (12-0, 9-0 Big Ten) hadn't "improved" in the weeks leading up to victories over Penn State and Wisconsin. A bye week followed.

"We asked," he said, "our guys to do more."

To the naked eye, Indiana appeared worn down, by the physical demands of six straight weeks without a break, plus the mental and emotional toll of chasing a season that's a lot rarer than most fans realize.

Cignetti suggested there had been just five Big Ten teams to complete a 12-0 season since 2000. It was too late, too dark and too cold for anyone to do the research to confirm or disprove his claim. *(Editor's fact-check: Indiana joined five other Big Ten teams to have gone 12-0 in the regular season since 2000: 2015 Iowa; 2017 Wisconsin; Ohio State in 2002, 2006, 2012, 2013 and 2019; Michigan in 2022 and 2023; and 2024 Oregon.)*

The fundamental point remained.

This kind of perfection is difficult. Arguably more so in the portal era. That difficulty was reflected in less-than-its-best IU performances across recent weeks.

Not this one. Not the 100th time the bitter rivals played for the Bucket.

Linebacker Aiden Fisher and coach Curt Cignetti walk off with the Old Oaken Bucket for the second straight season. The combined score from the 2024 and 2025 rivalry games: Indiana 122, Purdue 3. GRACE HOLLARS/INDYSTAR

HOOSIERS
adidas

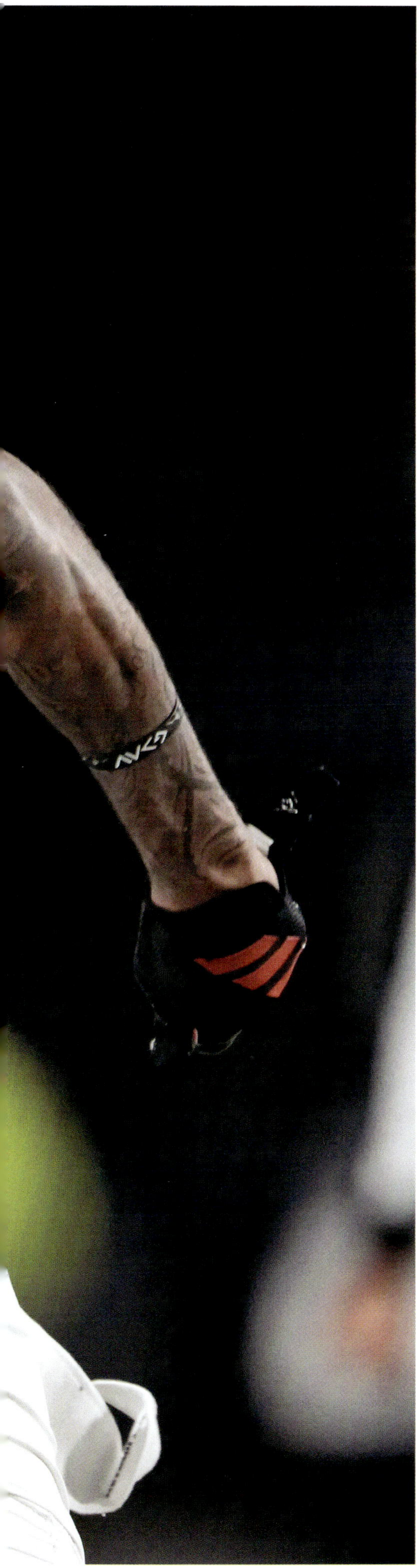

Indiana led 28-3 at halftime and just loped away from there. The Hoosiers rushed for 355 yards. Four players found the end zone on the ground (Kaelon Black, Roman Hemby, Khobie Martin and Fernando Mendoza). By the end, Indiana had freshmen handing off to freshmen and still pounded its way through a helpless Purdue defense.

The Hoosiers passed only 17 times, enough for three touchdowns (two from the Heisman candidate and one from little brother Alberto Mendoza).

When the Hoosiers were through, they celebrated retaining the Bucket with Cignetti, with their fans, with each other. Most fans for Purdue (2-10, 0-9) left long before the final quarter, numbed by the cold, deflated by the score and fearful of the forecast for a major snowstorm.

The Hoosiers never had recorded a perfect regular season. Their best came in 1945 with a 9-0-1 record, the only time IU won an outright Big Ten title. They were 9-2 in 1967, the only time IU shared (with Purdue and Minnesota) a conference title.

Cignetti admitted there was a fair bit of cigar smoke hanging in their locker room late Friday night.

"There's a lot of celebrating going on in that locker room right now," he said. "They're having a good old time. But they also understand they get to enjoy it for 24 hours. They understand, it's a great night for Indiana."

That's his general rule: Twenty-four hours to enjoy a victory, then it's on to the next thing.

The Hoosiers would need at least that long to start properly scouting their Big Ten championship game opponent — the next afternoon's results would determine whether it would be No. 1 Ohio State, No. 5 Oregon or No. 15 Michigan.

As for their path to Lucas Oil Stadium in Indianapolis, the Hoosiers left no doubt.

"We wanted to walk out of this game with an exclamation point, and not a question mark," Cignetti said, "and we did."

His team walked out with more than that. As Indiana's team buses pulled away, they did so with history onboard.

Not just a footnote or a career best. But the kind of thing that lasts forever, stamped in bronze and frozen permanently in the memory of a fan base living through the best days of its program's existence.

For Indiana football, these are most certainly the glory days. Cignetti had those 12-0 Big Ten teams at the ready when he referenced the number. Michigan here, Ohio State there. Oregon last year.

"Indiana, now," Cignetti said, adding his trademark wink. "Add them to the list."

Add them to the list. Forever. It can get better than this, but not by much. ■

Wide receiver Elijah Sarratt hunts for running room in the 100th clash for the Old Oaken Bucket on a bitterly cold Friday night. GRACE HOLLARS/INDYSTAR

THE B1G TITLE

GRACE SMITH/INDYSTAR

BIG TEN CHAMPIONSHIP • NO. 2 INDIANA 13, NO. 1 OHIO STATE 10
DECEMBER 6, 2025 • INDIANAPOLIS, INDIANA

UNDISPUTED AND UNBEATEN!

HOOSIERS EARN FIRST OUTRIGHT TITLE SINCE 1945 AND NO. 1 RANKING EVER

BY MICHAEL NIZIOLEK

Despite winning all its games by an average of 36½ points, Indiana came to Lucas Oil Stadium as the battle-tested team.

The second-ranked Hoosiers had pulled out a series of hard-earned victories on the road — at Iowa, Oregon and Penn State. Before the Big Ten championship game, top-ranked Ohio State hadn't trailed in the second half.

Those different journeys to Indianapolis helped determine the outcome of a hard-fought, nail-biting, emotional battle between the country's last unbeaten teams. In the final minutes, Indiana came through with clutch plays at every turn while Ohio State couldn't find the end zone after reaching the IU 9, missed a gimme field goal badly and couldn't get off the field on an IU third-and-6.

Indiana 13, Ohio State 10!

"No doubt about it," IU coach Curt Cignetti said. "I think we probably all on the bench — as that clock started to tick down into the fourth quarter and it was game on the line — probably at some point felt like, 'Wow, we've been here and we've won, and they've never been here.'"

In the latest history-making moment for a program that finished 3-9 two seasons ago, the Hoosiers beat Ohio State for the first time since 1988, won their first Big Ten title since sharing it with Purdue and Minnesota in 1967, and captured their first outright conference crown since 1945. The Hoosiers (13-0) also were guaranteed to ascend to the top of the polls for the first time ever, land the No. 1 seed in the 12-team College Football Playoff, earn a first-round bye and play their quarterfinal at the Rose Bowl on New Year's Day.

"We've accomplished a lot," Cignetti said. "You can't diminish what we've accomplished."

The road to Indianapolis was paved by making a key defensive stand at Iowa to force a late field goal that the Hawkeyes missed and then scoring on a 49-yard pass, rebounding after a fourth-quarter pick-six at Oregon with a 75-yard touchdown drive that took 6:19, and covering 80 yards in 75 seconds at Penn State thanks to an end-zone catch for the ages.

The stakes were never higher than Saturday night in downtown Indianapolis, but the Hoosiers had a steady pulse on their sideline.

"When you've been through something one time, you're a lot better the second time," Cignetti said. "Gives you a lot of belief and confidence."

That's how Indiana's defense survived two long OSU drives in the second half without surrendering a single point.

Midway through the third quarter, after IU went ahead 13-10 on Nico Radicic's 32-yard field goal, the Buckeyes (12-1) kept the ball for 6:28 and used 11 plays to travel 70 yards to the IU 5. On the 12th play, a fourth-and-1, Justin Sayin surged into a mass of humanity on a sneak for a first down — until a video review reversed the call on the field.

After a nine-play IU drive stalled, the Buckeyes started from their 10 with 10:45 left in the game. On OSU's 12th play, an 8-yard run by Bo Jackson made it second-and-2 from the IU 10 with 3:37 remaining. But defensive tackle Dominique Ratcliff and friends stopped Jackson's next rush at the 9. On third down, when Sayin rolled right and fired to tight end Bennett Christian in the end zone, linebacker Rolijah Hardy leaped and with his right arm deflected the ball a nanosecond before it could reach Christian's hands.

On fourth-and-1 with 2:51 left, OSU coach Ryan Day

Safety Louis Moore, who returned to Bloomington after a season with Ole Miss, holds the spoils from his sixth interception of the season. He ended Ohio State's opening drive by picking off Julian Sayin. Six plays later, Indiana took a 3-0 lead. RICH JANZARUK/HERALD-TIMES

HOOSIERS
7
OSIERS
4
HOOSIERS
46

elected to go for the tie. Jayden Fielding, who had missed only two kicks all season, pushed a 27-yard field-goal attempt way wide left.

"We had to find a way, they were like 12-play drives, and we just had to dig," IU defensive lineman Tyrique Tucker. "All of us had to dig and find a way to win. I was pretty gassed, but when it's championship ball, you can't be gassed. Still had to get after them."

It echoed the message Cignetti delivered to the team at the end of the extended halftime.

"I kind of gathered them right at the beginning of the end of the half, which I usually don't do, and very calmly said, this is what we talked about, this is the kind of game we expected," Cignetti said. "I gathered the team 20 minutes later, before we went out, it was more like, 'OK, do we have what it takes to win a gut check, physical game like this? This is going to be a test of our toughness and our persistence."

After the defense forced a three-and-out to start the third quarter, Indiana scored the game's only touchdown on a seven-play, 88-yard drive. Fernando Mendoza hit Charlie Becker for a 51-yard gain — one of the longest plays OSU had surrendered all season — setting up a 17-yard touchdown throw to Elijah Sarratt.

Day later said he regretted not attempting a field goal when Sayin was stopped on fourth-and-1 in the third quarter, but he thought going for the tie in the fourth quarter was the right move.

"When you miss a field goal," Day said, "you're sick over it and you second-guess yourself right from the jump."

He later said: "We were struggling down there in the red area, and let's get the thing tied up and see if we can get the ball back and look to kick a field goal to win the game."

After Fielding's miss, the Hoosiers quickly faced a third-and-6 from their 24 with 2:41 left. But Mendoza connected with Becker in one-on-one coverage for an over-the-shoulder, 33-yard catch.

There were times earlier this season that Mendoza put the ball in harm's way in big moments, but that didn't happen against the Buckeyes.

"When the game was on the line, you know, Fernando was throwing dimes," Cignetti said.

OSU finally got the ball back at its 10 with 18 seconds left.

The championship game marked a reversal from when the teams crossed paths in Columbus in 2024 and IU collapsed under all the pressure in a 38-15 defeat. Cignetti even told reporters heading into the title game that he felt the moment was "too big" for the Hoosiers in 2024.

Those comments gave IU's locker room added motivation to show their coach they had learned all the right lessons this season.

"All of us wanted to go out there," Tucker said, "and put a stamp on the season." ■

— Gene Myers contributed.

'THE HOOSIERS ARE FLIPPIN' CHAMPS'

BY NAT NEWELL

Moments after Indiana defeated Ohio State for its first outright Big Ten championship in 80 years, Fox's Jenny Taft grabbed quarterback Fernando Mendoza for an on-field interview. His adrenaline-fueled response blew up the internet.

"It sounds so beautiful," Mendoza told Taft, his voice cracking, eyes fixed on the camera, bordering on hyperventilation and approaching tears. "I want to give all the glory to God. We were never supposed to be in this position, but by the glory of God, the great coaches, great teammates, everyone we have around us, we were able to pull it off. Whoever thought the Hoosiers would be here now? The Hoosiers are flippin' champs. Let's go!"

Over the weekend, Mendoza told ABC News: "I was overwhelmed by raw and genuine emotion. Maybe I might have shown too much emotion, maybe too much direct eye contact into the camera; however, it was what was genuine and authentic to myself at that moment. Beating the No. 1 team in the nation, Ohio State, was such a great accomplishment for my teammates and I."

Wide receiver Elijah Sarratt celebrates one of the season's biggest catches: a 17-yard touchdown pass from Fernando Mendoza that pushed Indiana ahead of Ohio State 13-10 with 8:30 left in the third quarter. No more points were scored in the game. RICH JANZARUK/HERALD-TIMES

13
BIG
HOOSIERS

THE BEST TEAM, PLAYER AND COACH: CIGNETTI SPEAKS IMPOSSIBLE INTO EXISTENCE WITH BIG TEN TITLE AND TOPPLING TOP-RANKED OHIO STATE

BY GREGG DOYEL

Indiana football players are wearing these huge red T-shirts — "2025 Big Ten champions," the shirts say — and running around the field at Lucas Oil Stadium, trying to dodge confetti and each other and failing at all of it and not caring, not even a little bit. Some of them are using the confetti to make snow angels on the field. Others are running through the end zone and trying to leap into the deliriously happy Hoosiers crowd.

And there on the field, alone with his thoughts and his athletic director, is coach Curt Cignetti. He's just standing there next to Scott Dolson, looking around, taking in the aftermath of the second-ranked Hoosiers' 13-10 victory over top-ranked Ohio State in the Big Ten championship game.

What could he possibly be thinking about? By defeating Ohio State (12-1), the Hoosiers (13-0) had become the last undefeated team — and positioned themselves to earn the first No. 1 ranking in program history when the US LBM Coaches Poll, Associated Press media poll and College Football Playoff rankings come out the next afternoon. His quarterback, Fernando Mendoza, had just won the Grange-Griffin Trophy as the game's MVP and positioned himself to win the Heisman Trophy, the first in IU history. And Cignetti, without question, should sweep national coach of the year awards.

This was IU football, circa 2023: The losingest program in college football history.

This is IU football, circa 2025: Best team, best player, best coach in the country.

So, there's Cignetti, just standing there quietly, away from the action, when his private moment goes public thanks to a stadium camera that transmits his blank face onto the gigantic videoboard. The crowd doesn't see it, not at first — fans are busy watching IU players making snow angels and running laps around the place — but soon the fans spot their coach on the scoreboard. The crowd has been cheering this whole time, but here comes the real noise.

What Hoosiers fans just watched is the culmination of an impossible dream, a series of preposterous boasts by Cignetti nearly two years ago to the day. He just been had hired from James Madison, and his mouth hit the ground running. Remember? Google me, he said. Purdue sucks, he said. But so do Michigan and Ohio State, he said.

And then, of course, he had said this on Dec. 1, 2023, the day after he had accepted the job, when he was invited to Lucas Oil Stadium 24 hours before the 2023 Big Ten title game. Remember what he said?

"I figured I had to make this trip up here," Cignetti said, "since we'll be playing in this game next year."

Almost. The 2024 team didn't qualify for the Big Ten title game, but it did go 11-2 and reach the College Football Playoff. One year later, on an electric Saturday night in downtown Indianapolis, the Hoosiers were playing in this game. And winning it. And positioning themselves for a starring role —playing themselves — in the college football version of the movie "Hoosiers."

So, what does Cignetti say when Fox's Joel Klatt asks for his thoughts on his program's shocking rise to the top?

"I think we're a year late," Cignetti said.

This guy.

MENDOZA OUTDUELS SAYIN, CLINCHES HEISMAN TROPHY

The game started terribly for Indiana. Like, this was a nightmare, and it was inflicted by a local kid from Center Grove. His name is Caden Curry, a senior defensive end

Defensive tackle Mario Landino and quarterback Fernando Mendoza embrace the moment at Lucas Oil Stadium: The Hoosiers won the Big Ten championship game for the first time. RICH JANZARUK/HERALD-TIMES

97
15

for the Buckeyes, and on the first play from scrimmage he smashes into Mendoza and leaves him lying there, face down, not moving at the 20-yard line.

Mendoza doesn't look conscious. Not sure he's even alive, not for 30 seconds, until he sits up. Finally, he trudges off the field, but this is no good. Obviously, he's not going to come back any time soon, so his backup — his kid brother, Alberto Mendoza — comes into the game and hands off to Roman Hemby, and the result is a first down. The crowd erupts, and really, it's a bit much for a first down, but ...

Wait. Mendoza is coming back into the game? Already?

Fernando Mendoza?

He's running to the huddle and the crowd is joyful, and while the Hoosiers barely cross midfield on their first drive, catastrophe has been avoided. But not Curry. He continues to pound away at Mendoza, sacking him twice and whacking him to the turf another time and even breaking up a pass at the line of scrimmage. Caden Curry has made himself some NFL cash in this game.

Mendoza? He's still in the game, but he's 3-for-8 with the weirdest interception ever, a wide receiver screen intended for Elijah Sarratt that glances off the back of the tight end in the area, Riley Nowakowski, and into the hands of cornerback Davison Igbinosun. The Hoosiers kick an early field goal, then miss one — Nico Radicic's first miss of the season, after making his first 70 PATs and his first 14 field goals — and Ohio State scores once, then twice, to take a 10-3 lead.

This game started terribly, but the Hoosiers are hanging around, and they're doing it without their most talented receiver. Omar Cooper Jr. had hopped off the field on the first drive, five plays after Mendoza's injury, and didn't return. Ohio State has won 30 consecutive games against the Hoosiers and are on a 60-2-2 run in the all-time series, but the game drags on and it becomes apparent:

The Buckeyes have met their match. And it's Indiana!

Sorry. It's, um, Indiana.

The IU defense is limiting the OSU running game to 58 yards on 26 carries. OSU quarterback Julian Sayin, Mendoza's only remaining competition for the Heisman, is having a mediocre game despite all the NFL talent in his receiving corps (Jeremiah Smith and Carnell Tate) and tight end room (Purdue transfer Max Klare).

And don't look now, but Mendoza is getting hot.

After his 3-for-8 start, he finishes the games on a 12-for-15 heater, with gains of 51 and 33 yards to Charlie Becker and a gorgeous 17-yard back-shoulder fade to Sarratt for a touchdown. IU owns a 13-10 lead midway through the third quarter.

Ohio State answers with an eight-minute drive that falls short when the IU defense turns back Sayin on a sneak on fourth-and-1 inside the Indiana 5.

Now the third quarter is over, and the pro-Hoosiers crowd — I'm calling it 60-40, Indiana — is starting to believe, and Pat McAfee is about to do what he does and take things over the top.

MCAFEE LIGHTS UP IU FANS WITH HIS MINI-STRIPTEASE

You've got to hand it to the folks running the cameras at Lucas Oil Stadium: They know where to go. There was the Cignetti shot after the game, of course, but before that came the break between the third and fourth quarters, when the cameras are panning the stadium, searching the crowd for something interesting — and there's McAfee, sitting in his box behind one end zone. Pretty sure that's Indiana Pacers star Tyrese Haliburton sitting next to him, but McAfee blots out everyone and everything by reacting to the camera this way:

Hopping to his feet, ripping off his tank top, twirling it around and around and then leading the crowd into the chant, the moment, they've been awaiting for decades:

Hoo-hoo-hoo ... HOO-SIERS!

The place is on fire, and poor Ohio State kicker Jayden Fielding is a sacrificial offering. Fielding has been almost perfect this season as well, going 16-for-18 on field goals and 54-for-54 on extra points, and he's lining up for a 27-yard chip shot, but Lucas Oil Stadium is electric and hostile and he pulls the chip shot low and left with 2:48 left, and that will just about do it.

All Indiana needs is one first down, and look at Cignetti, calling a deep pass play on third-and-6 at his 24. And look at Becker (six catches, 126 yards), who had seven catches in the first nine games but has had three 100-yard performances in the last five games, getting behind the OSU secondary. And look at Mendoza, lobbing a perfectly precise pass to Becker for 33 yards.

On a makeshift stage, wide receiver Elijah Sarratt sports a championship medal and T-shirt while quarterback Fernando Mendoza holds the Grange-Griffin Trophy as the MVP of the title game. RICH JANZARUK/HERALD-TIMES

Now it's over, and we wait for the final CFP bracket reveal. The Hoosiers will get the top seed, a first-round bye and play a New Year's Day quarterfinal at the Rose Bowl.

And Cignetti's already thinking ahead. Remember his reaction to being in the program's first Big Ten title game, and winning it?

"I think we're a year late."

So here's his reaction to whatever comes next, as he told Fox's Klatt — and the Lucas Oil Stadium crowd — after this one was over.

"Hey," he said, "I got two things to say — besides all the thank-yous to the president, Pam Whitten, the AD, Scott Dolson, our assistant coaches, our team, our seniors, our fans, all right?

"We're Big Ten champions! You talk about changing the way people think — I got 3½ weeks to get this team humble and hungry for the playoffs."

The crowd roared some more, because if there's one thing they've learned in the last two years, it's this: When Curt Cignetti puts his mind to it, he can speak the impossible into existence. ■

THE HEISMAN

GRACE HOLLARS/INDYSTAR

HEIS-MENDOZA! HEIS-MENDOZA!

LAPPING THE FIELD, MENDOZA WINS FIRST HOOSIER HEISMAN

BY GREGG DOYEL | DECEMBER 13, 2025

Indiana quarterback Fernando Mendoza bounds up the stairs in New York City, as happy as you can imagine. He's smiling wide and every eye in the place is on him — everyone knows exactly who he is — but this is what he says: "How you guys doing? I'm Fernando Mendoza."

Hey, you're right: You watched the Heisman Trophy presentation show Saturday night on ABC, and that's not exactly what happened there.

But who said I was talking about the Heisman Trophy presentation? That was a foregone conclusion. "Fernando Mendoza for Heisman" has been trending that way since Oct. 18, when Mendoza led the Hoosiers to a 38-13 victory against Michigan State and fans at Memorial Stadium started the chant that became the best Heisman Trophy campaign in, I don't know, forever?

Heis-Mendoza!

Heis-Mendoza!

A chant that good takes off, takes on a life of its own, becomes a #Heismendoza hashtag and even gets its own LinkedIn page, for crying out loud. And then when Mendoza follows it up by leading the Hoosiers to the Big Ten title, the first No. 1 ranking in program history and the last remaining perfect record in major-college football, the Heisman race is over. And not because he's the best player on the country's best team — though he is — but the country's best player.

Mendoza goes into the College Football Playoff leading the country in touchdown passes (33), ranking third in passer rating (181.4) and seventh in accuracy (71.5%) and sitting as the presumptive No. 1 overall pick in the NFL draft. He ranks "just" 24th nationally in passing yards (2,980) but for good reason: He has been too good. The Hoosiers didn't lose, as I said, and were rarely pushed. Average final score: Indiana 42-11. The Hoosiers won six games by at least 45 points. Hard to throw for a ton of yards when you're sitting out so many fourth quarters.

Anyway, the Heisman Trophy has belonged to Mendoza for weeks. Saturday night was a foregone conclusion, as I said.

Saturday morning? That was unexpected. About 10 hours before the Heisman Trophy presentation at Jazz at Lincoln Center, Mendoza was bounding up the stairs of an Adidas store in Manhattan, where he had invited four families affected by Multiple Sclerosis — Mendoza's mother, Elsa, battles MS — to experience a $10,000 shopping spree courtesy of Mendoza and Adidas.

The families are waiting at the top of the stairs, all those moms and dads and children staring as the best player on the best team in college football ascends with a smile as sparkling, as pure as his all-white IU jumpsuit.

Mendoza being Mendoza — and by that I mean: one of the humblest superstars in college football history — he assumes nothing.

"How you guys doing?" Mendoza tells the families. "I'm Fernando Mendoza. Thank you, guys, so much for coming today. I really appreciate it and really hope you guys have a good time today."

That's how Mendoza spent time before becoming the first Heisman Trophy winner in Hoosiers history — serving others.

Yeah, you know what? You're right:

That should've been a foregone conclusion, too.

THE HISTORIC MOMENT FOR INDIANA FOOTBALL

When his name is finally announced, in the 61st minute of the scheduled one-hour show, Mendoza closes his eyes

After an hour-plus presentation show in New York, Fernando Mendoza poses for posterity with the Heisman Trophy, one of sport's most iconic awards. In its first 90 years, no Hoosier had won it. Running back Anthony Thompson finished second in 1989. BRAD PENNER/IMAGN IMAGES

PREMIER PARTNER
THE HEISMAN MEMORIAL TROPHY
PRESENTED BY
THE HEISMAN TROPHY TRUST
TO
FERNANDO MENDOZA
INDIANA UNIVERSITY
AS THE OUTSTANDING COLLEGE FOOTBALL PLAYER
IN THE UNITED STATES FOR
2025

and purses his lips. He's trying not to cry, but he's going to be like so many others in that room and fail miserably.

This was emotional because Mendoza is an emotional guy and — more than that — a wonderful guy. It showed during his moment on stage during the buildup to the announcement, when he and coach Curt Cignetti were introduced to the crowd, and ESPN's Holly Rowe mentioned Cignetti's haul of coach of the year trophies. The room goes silent. Nobody claps. Not the crowd, not the past Heisman winners on stage, nobody.

Nobody but Fernando Mendoza.

Rowe encourages the crowd to do what IU has done all season, follow Mendoza, and the crowd does by applauding Cignetti. Rowe turns to the coach, who compares Mendoza to a guy from his home state of West Virginia — "Jerry West," Cignetti says, "known as Mr. Clutch" — and then lists the games where we saw it happen: "At Oregon, against Ohio State in the Big Ten championship game, the two-minute drive against Penn State, the fourth quarter at Iowa."

"Unbelievable," Cignetti continues. "He plays his best football in the clutch moments, when the pressure's on."

Now Cignetti is shifting his words to Fernando Mendoza, the person, how teammates loves him.

"A lot of layers to this guy, now," Cignetti says. "I take notes when he does interviews."

Here, Rowe goes completely off script and blurts, "I think he's the most impressive person I've ever met in my life."

Then Rowe asks Mendoza about the potential dream finish to this dream season, playing for the national championship in his hometown of Miami. It's a dangerous question — how do you answer that, off the cuff? — but here's how Mendoza handles it: By turning his attention to the Hoosiers' next game (Jan. 1 at the Rose Bowl), then complimenting the two teams who will play each other for the right to face IU (Alabama and Oklahoma) before acknowledging, yes, the dream of playing for a title in Miami ... and then bringing his focus back to the Rose Bowl.

"Are we all taking notes?" Rowe asks the crowd. "Most impressive young man ever."

We'll see more of it when Mendoza wins the trophy and starts his acceptance speech and vows to the Heisman winners in the room to "carry the Heisman name with humility." He thanks Hoosier Nation, coaches, teammates, offense, defense and even breaks down the offense by position group:

"To my linemen who protected me, every receiver and tight end who bailed me out and made me look good, every running back who fought for more yards ..."

He thanks his younger brother, redshirt freshman quarterback Alberto Mendoza — he's got next — and his high school coach and Christopher Columbus High itself. He thanks the university he left after the 2024 season, California, "for being the first to believe in me."

Now he's moving onto his youngest brother, Max, who's bawling, and his mom, who's crying, and his dad, who's sniffling. He shifts to Spanish to thank his grandparents, first-generation Cuban immigrants, and while I don't know much Spanish, I know this:

"Yo quiero mucho," he tells them.

Next, a shout-out to Coach Cig: "You drove me to a level I didn't even know I had in me."

Mendoza saves his last comments for strangers, for kids he doesn't know, the kids watching this show and are certain, just certain, they will never be good enough to be on that stage someday.

Wrong, Mendoza wants those kids to know.

"This is an important one," he says. "I want every kid out there who feels overlooked, underestimated, to know I ... was ... you. I was that kid, too. I was in your shoes. The truth is, you don't need the most (recruiting) stars, hype or ranking. You just need discipline, heart and people who believe in you. And you need to believe in your own abilities. I hope this moment shows that chasing your dreams is worth it."

It showed that. And more.

AN ALL-TIME GREAT PERSON ON AND OFF THE FIELD FOR IU

Maybe we've seen Heisman Trophy winners with more swag, better stats, bigger NFL hype. But have we ever seen a Heisman Trophy winner of more significance off the field?

It's not just this, but fine, let's start here:

Has there even been a nicer, more socially aware Heisman Trophy winner? You saw what happened Saturday

The four finalists hope to hoist, not just touch, college football's biggest prize. From the left: Notre Dame running back Jeremiyah Love, Indiana quarterback Fernando Mendoza, Vanderbilt quarterback Diego Pavia and Ohio State quarterback Julian Sayin. BRAD PENNER/IMAGN IMAGES

HOW THEY FARED ...

Indiana quarterback Fernando Mendoza easily outdistanced the field to win the 91st Heisman Trophy. He was the first player since USC's Caleb Williams in 2022 to finish first in all six of the award's geographic regions. The top 10:

PLAYER/POSITION/SCHOOL	FIRST	SECOND	THIRD	POINTS
Fernando Mendoza, QB, Indiana	643	191	51	2,362
Diego Pavia, QB, Vanderbilt	189	352	164	1,435
Jeremiyah Love, RB, Notre Dame	46	157	267	719
Julian Sayin, QB, Ohio State	8	118	172	432
Jacob Rodriguez, LB, Texas Tech	17	56	132	295
Jeremiah Smith, WR, Ohio State	4	18	36	84
Gunner Stockton, QB, Georgia	3	6	22	43
Trinidad Chambliss, QB, Ole Miss	2	5	7	23
Caleb Downs, S, Ohio State	2	3	10	22
Haynes King, QB, Georgia Tech	2	1	10	18

night. That's who he is, who he always has been. Mendoza has used his platform to help raise more than $100,000 for various National Multiple Sclerosis Society campaigns. At Christopher Columbus High School in Miami, he was that kid who gives so much of himself, you wonder how he has time for trigonometry class.

Mendoza was president of Campus Ministry, vice president of his class and social media director for the honors program while at CCHS. He organized the school's annual turkey drive, coming up with 436 turkeys for families in need in Dade County. The grandson of Cuban immigrants, he organized a trip to Cuba with his maternal grandmother and did charity work with local churches and elementary schools there.

At IU, Mendoza's on-field postgame interviews have become must-see national television. He thanks God, coaches, teammates and the TV network. He congratulates the other team on a hard-fought game, and if was played on the road, he compliments the opposing crowd.

And he means it.

Mendoza is so genuine, nearly a dozen teammates paid their way to New York to celebrate his Heisman Trophy — foregone conclusion, remember? — and so loyal, in return, that he has decided the Heisman Trophy won't follow him to the NFL.

"I'd want to keep the trophy in Bloomington because it belongs there," Mendoza told reporters, including our Michael Niziolek, before the ceremony. "That's what I think as far as everything Hoosier Nation has done for me, if I have the honor and blessing of winning it.

"I think it would mean so much for the fan base that has stuck through the thick and thin to now the Cignetti era."

This is where Mendoza's skyrocketing off-field impact heads for territory somewhere off the charts: What has he done for IU football?

True, this movement started last year with Cignetti, who this week swept (again) the Walter Camp and Home Depot Coach of the Year awards, becoming the first to win consecutive Walter Camp honors in the award's 59-year history.

Cignetti got this party started, but how much juice has Mendoza given the Hoosiers by adding the iconic Heisman to his earlier trophies? He also won the Davey O'Brien Award, Maxwell Award and Walter Camp Award and leads the bracket's No. 1 seed into a New Year's Day quarterfinal. He has become the likely No. 1 pick in the draft.

While Cignetti has shown what the IU football program can do, Mendoza has shown what an IU player can do. The transfer portal brims with players wanting to come to Bloomington and become the next Mendoza, or Aiden Fisher, or Elijah Sarratt, or Pat Coogan, or ...

The possibilities are endless, now that Fernando Mendoza has won the first Heisman Trophy in IU history, doing the impossible — and turning it into a foregone conclusion. ■

Above: Fernando Mendoza poses with families dealing with MS. They received shopping sprees at the Adidas flagship store in New York, located a few blocks from the National MS Society's headquarters. MICHAEL NIZIOLEK/HERALD-TIMES

Opposite: Fernando Mendoza goes through a media gauntlet at the New York Marriott Marquis before the Heisman Trophy presentation ceremony. More than 100 friends, teammates, coaches and family members attended an afterparty at Elsie Rooftop. BRAD PENNER/IMAGN IMAGES

THE GLORY

GRACE HOLLARS/INDYSTAR

COLLEGE FOOTBALL PLAYOFF ROSE BOWL • NO. 1 INDIANA 38, NO. 9 ALABAMA 3
JANUARY 1, 2026 • PASADENA, CALIFORNIA

ROSES ARE CRIMSON

HOOSIERS ROUT ALABAMA FOR FIRST ROSE BOWL VICTORY

BY MICHAEL NIZIOLEK

No. 1 Indiana won the Rose Bowl in dominant fashion — 38-3 over No. 9 Alabama, a sentence that needs no embellishment for significance.

It says everything required.

The unbeaten Hoosiers will have little time to stop and smell the roses — no time if Curt Cignetti had his way. Their first Rose Bowl victory (IU lost to USC on Jan. 1, 1968, their other Pasadena appearance) sends Indiana to the Peach Bowl in Atlanta on Jan. 9 for a rematch against No. 5 Oregon with a berth in the national championship game on the line.

In the Granddaddy of Them All, Indiana (14-0) bucked the trend of higher seeds falling flat after lengthy layoffs. Higher seeds with first-round byes in the new 12-team playoff were 0-6 heading into Jan. 1's games.

In other firsts for anyone who Googles Cignetti: IU won its first game ever on New Year's Day, its first bowl since the 1991 Copper Bowl and its third bowl in 14 trips.

After a scoreless first quarter — although IU outgained Alabama 79-18 and Fernando Mendoza was 6-for-6 passing — Nico Radcic kicked a 31-yard field goal to open the second quarter. Four plays later came the game's initial turning point.

Facing fourth-and-1 from their 34, the Crimson Tide lined up in a wildcat formation. Coach Ken DeBoer later said he hadn't decided whether to go for it but wanted to try a hard count for an offside penalty while his staff concocted a potential fourth-down play. Instead, Cignetti called a time-out with the play clock at five seconds.

Alabama then lined up in punt formation, which included quarterback Ty Simpson as a personal protector, but quickly shifted in a bizarre tight formation with Simpson under center but punter Blake Doud still 15 yards behind the line of scrimmage. Simpson bopped around and tried to draw a penalty, but when the Hoosiers didn't budge, DeBoer called a time-out right before the play clock expired. TV cameras caught Simpson smiling as he headed to the sideline.

Time to punt, right? Nope. The Tide lined up with running back Daniel Hill in a wildcat and Simpson split out wide with receiver Germie Bernard. Bernard headed in motion to his left, Hill received the snap, Hill popped the ball to Bernard, and Bernard tried to turn the edge. He was met by linebackers Isaiah Jones and Rolijah Hardy and then shoved backward with help from five of their friends.

"It definitely was a point where we had them shook a little bit," defensive end Mikail Kamara said.

Despite all of Alabama shenanigans, Kamara said linebacker Aiden Fisher called out where the ball was going before the snap

"They tried to get us with the hard count; we didn't jump for it," Kamara said. "Then, they still decided to go for it. They tried to run a crazy jet play, and we stuffed it. It was like, 'Yeah, we can win this game.'"

DeBoer explained his thinking: "I try not to be reckless but try to be aggressive. ... I really felt like, after that point, I was committed to going for it and wanting to try to make it happen."

What happened 107 seconds later was a 10-0 deficit for the Tide. After an IU holding penalty, Roman Hemby ran for 21 yards, Hemby ran for two more yards, Mendoza

Linebacker Aiden Fisher can't make coach Curt Cignetti stop, but he can make him smell the roses as he hoists the Leishman Trophy. Rose Bowl awards went to center Pat Coogan (offensive MVP) and cornerback D'Angelo Ponds (defensive MVP). GRACE HOLLARS/INDYSTAR

4

and Charlie Becker couldn't connect at the 11, and Becker made an impressive leaping grab on a 21-yard pass in the end zone, coming down in a near somersault.

Mendoza's 1-yard pass to Omar Cooper Jr., returning from a leg injury in the Big Ten title game, made the lead 17-0 with 17 seconds left in the half. Cooper finished with three catches for 45 yards.

Even though Alabama erased a 17-point deficit in the first round against Oklahoma, Indiana didn't allow even a glimmer of hope.

"We knew the rest of the game they had to pass the ball," Kamara said. "That's basically like a third down on every single play, and we are the best third-down defense. It was honestly playing into our hand and what we do best."

They pressured Simpson on six of his 19 drop backs, per Pro Football Focus. He also didn't have success scrambling out of the pocket as he did against previous opponents.

Simpson fumbled at the end of the second quarter and took a hit from cornerback D'Angelo Ponds on the play that ultimately knocked him out of the game with a rib injury. He was replaced by Austin Mack, who was sacked three times, after Simpson played the opening series of the second half.

Alabama only crossed the 40-yard line twice and its lone trip in the red zone resulted in a field goal on a drive that stalled at the 10.

Alabama's 193 yards marked its lowest output since a victory over Tulane in 2008. Thanks to 25 yards lost via the sacks, the Tide managed only 23 yards rushing on 17 carries.

Indiana gained 215 yards on the ground, led by 99 yards and a TD by Kaelon Black and 89 yards and a TD by Hemby.

Because of the Hoosiers' ground game — with 50 rushes — center Pat Coogan was selected the game's offensive MVP.

"He embodies what this program is about, even though it's his first year here," said offensive coordinator Mike Shanahan. "His leadership has been invaluable."

The defensive MVP went to Ponds, who provided blanket coverage to go with his forced fumble and three tackles. ■

— Zach Osterman and Gene Myers contributed.

Fernando Mendoza cradles the Leishman Trophy on a makeshift stage at the Rose Bowl. He was a picture of efficiency: 14 of 16 passing for 192 yards and three touchdowns. GRACE HOLLARS/INDYSTAR

ROSE BOWL GAME
presented by
Prudential
INDIAN

'IT'LL BE A HELL OF A MOVIE': INDIANA'S METEORIC RISE HAS BECOME COLLEGE FOOTBALL'S GREATEST STORY, ONE WE WILL NEVER SEE AGAIN

BY ZACH OSTERMAN

How to explain all this? The historical improbability of it. The casual dominance of it. The unrelenting, singular excellence of it. For two years, we've tried — and, as the stakes and the successes have increased, failed — to adequately explain what is happening in real time to Indiana football, the program now redefining virtually every convention we've come to hold about this sport.

It's time to stop addressing IU according to its past. That book is closed. The Hoosiers are now only what you see on the field: dominant, merciless and inevitable.

We don't allow ourselves to think that way anymore. Surely too much history has been made, too much has happened, for anything to be unique anymore. But it's oh so possible that this is: Indiana is authoring the greatest story in college football history, one it's time to stop asking anyone else to repeat, because this will never happen again.

"It'll be a hell of a movie," Curt Cignetti told ESPN's Rece Davis on stage accepting the Leishman Trophy given to the Rose Bowl winner.

The latest chapter in this remarkable tale, a 38-3 victory on New Year's Day, was among the most memorable. And for this fan base, the most important.

The opportunity mattered.

No team in the 12-team College Football Playoff format had won following a first-round bye. Until halftime Thursday, no team coming into the quarterfinal off a bye even had led at halftime.

No. 9 Alabama (11-4) stood no chance, it turned out, of continuing that trend.

The upset-minded Crimson Tide — what a collection of words that is in this context — talked about disrespect and doubt coming in. They drew fuel from these things, they said. They relished being counted out against dominant, darling Indiana (14-0), the No. 1 team in the country.

And for all the good it did them — they wound up where 13 other opponents had, shattered against the unbreakable rock that had become Indiana. Under Cignetti, there was no better coached, more prepared, more aligned, more detail-oriented team in America.

And for those reasons, there's a very good chance there was none better, period.

"You've just got to tip your hat to Indiana," Alabama coach Kalen DeBoer said, joining a long list in his profession left no other choice. "They execute. They just execute at a high level, and everyone feeds off each other on both sides of the ball.

"It's not just one thing."

It's not just one thing, and because of that, it's everything.

How often has Indiana been outplayed in any phase of football in a single game? When, across the last 14 games, has an opponent outplayed the Hoosiers between the sidelines for 60 minutes offensively, defensively or on special teams?

Penn State for maybe 20 minutes of that second half. Iowa, maybe, for a moment. That's the list.

Forget for a moment the history or the helmets. That measure of dominance is remarkable. It is not unprecedented, but it's supposed to be all but impossible in this era of parity and talent diaspora.

These Hoosiers hold greater ambitions than were realized under a cloudy Pasadena sky. But the Rose Bowl remains

Kaelon Black dashes past Alabama's first line of defense en route to a 15 carry, 99-yard Rose Bowl. He scored on a 25-yard run in the fourth quarter. Minus sack and kneel-down yardage, IU gained 243 yards on the ground. GRACE HOLLARS/INDYSTAR

ROSE BOWL GAME
presented by
Prudential
B1G
CFP2026
BATTLE

— for at least one more year — a place of pilgrimage for any Big Ten fan base, much less one for so long so desperate for this kind of success.

So, yes, the opportunity mattered.

So, too, did the opponent.

DeBoer could be forgiven feeling aggrieved at the extent to which this game became about good vs. evil. Alabama the team arrived in California with nothing but respect for IU and all its success.

Alabama the idea represented something unavoidable, though.

SEC vs. Big Ten bias colored this matchup because of two years of doubt and detraction. Every attempt to belittle or cheapen what Cignetti and his program have accomplished across the last two years.

This coach does not suffer lazy criticism, something he made clear with his SEC scheduling comments at media days in July. And his fan base has learned to embrace its coach's admirable recalcitrance in the face of a college football industrial complex that has attempted to shame Indiana into accepting it has no right to be this good.

There's only one way to answer that kind of criticism: Stuff it in the nearest available locker. Something these Hoosiers spent the summer and autumn doing time and again. They would not stop with the changing of the calendar.

"That's what you would always love to see as the head coach, things we used to preach when I was at Alabama," Cignetti said.

Cignetti referenced in the same answer "the best way to do it," a way familiar to interested observers by now. If one may be so bold, a most Sabanesque way.

Run downhill, with anger and force. Stay gap sound and angry on the other side of the ball. Make fewer mistakes. Make no mistakes. Grind your opponent into fine powder and let the 3- and 4-yard carries in the first half become explosives and touchdowns in the second.

"Changing the way they think," Cignetti said. "Breaking their will."

Indiana rushed for 215 net yards on 4.3 yards a carry. The Hoosiers' last two touchdowns came on rushes of 25 and 18 yards, Kaelon Black and Roman Hemby bursting through one-armed tackles and sprinting away from tired legs.

Indiana beat Alabama in the most recognizably Alabama way possible.

When the time came to hand out the offensive MVP award, teammates turned expectantly toward Fernando Mendoza. He was excellent Thursday, finishing with 233 sack-adjusted total yards, three touchdown passes and three rushing first downs.

But he was not the intended recipient of an honor that in its modern history had been reserved almost exclusively for skill players and quarterbacks.

No, that award went to Pat Coogan, Indiana's center. The shocked look on his face matched the shock that an offensive lineman in modern football could win this award.

"A credit to all my teammates," Coogan said. "These guys are unbelievable."

Here, Coogan was not quite right. Nothing about Indiana was unbelievable anymore.

This is the last and greatest of the Hoosiers' myriad remarkable qualities — they are the best team in America.

There can be no more doubt now. No denial made in good faith or worth taking seriously.

IU might not win a national title, because that's hard to do, and sometimes the other team shows up a little bit better on the day and the ball bounces wrong and injuries happen and so forth.

But this is now surely the best team in college football. It has the best quarterback. It has the best coach. It has the best defense and the best wins and the best story, and on and on and on.

Perhaps most importantly, after generations spent thirsting for just this moment, it has a fan base ready to meet it with arms wide and hearts full.

One of the peculiarities of Indiana's dominance these last two seasons — especially at home — has been that Hoosiers haven't really given their fans a moment. No last-minute victory. No field storming.

Maybe Indianapolis last month was that to some extent, but it felt as important to everyone on the field as off it. New Year's Day was different.

IU fans outnumbered their crimson counterparts at least 3 to 1 in the Rose Bowl stands, maybe more than that. And from the moment the teams ran out from their respective

Wide receiver Elijah Sarratt reaches out and touches the man of the hour on the Rose Bowl's makeshift stage. Center Pat Coogan, in his first season after transferring from Notre Dame, was selected the game's offensive MVP, a rare honor for an offensive lineman. GRACE HOLLARS/INDYSTAR

tunnels until they exited the same way, it sounded like it.

Of course, by the end of the fourth quarter, Alabama-minded folks had largely hit the exits. There was nothing left for them to see. The same could not be said for the thousands and thousands of Indiana fans with no intention of going anywhere.

Sometime around the two-minute time-out in the second half, someone on the stadium PA system queued up Journey's "Don't Stop Believin'," and IU fans made it clear they would not.

Streetlights, people
Livin' just to find emotion

Together, they did, a chorus collectively greeting its new world. Indiana football is nothing more or less now than what it has become, and what it emphatically remained into the new year — the justifiable envy of college football.

It is a remarkable story, maybe the best in the history of the sport, and certainly one we will never see again. ■

COLLEGE FOOTBALL PLAYOFF PEACH BOWL • NO. 1 INDIANA 56, NO. 5 OREGON 22
JANUARY 9, 2026 • ATLANTA, GEORGIA

DUCK SEASON AGAIN

REMATCH NO CONTEST; HOOSIERS ONE WIN FROM IMMORTALITY

BY MICHAEL NIZIOLEK AND NAT NEWELL

The Indiana Hoosiers stand one victory from the greatest rags-to-riches story in college football history.

The top-ranked Hoosiers bulldozed No. 5 Oregon 56-22 in the Peach Bowl with a pick-six on the game's first play, five touchdown passes from Fernando Mendoza, a blocked punt in the final quarter and Curt Cignetti smiling, laughing and delivering a one-liner during a postgame on-the-field interview.

Where to unravel as dominant of a performance as Indiana had put together in a season full of them? Not at the start — when D'Angelo Ponds read the quarterback's eyes, jumped a route and dashed 25 yards to the end zone 11 seconds into the game — but at the finish — when ESPN's Molly McGrath corralled Cignetti on the turf of Mercedes-Benz Stadium.

After 80 seconds of the usual coachspeak, McGrath touched on what figured to be an unpopular topic for the sideline-stoic, laser-focused coach: celebrating this victory instead of prepping for the national championship game Jan. 19 against 10th-seeded Miami (Florida) at Hard Rock Stadium, the Hurricanes' home field.

"Coach, I know you're thinking about the next game," McGrath said, "but when will you stop and appreciate how special and how historic all of this has been?"

"I'm really not thinking about the next game," Cignetti said with a deadpan. "I'm thinking about cracking open a beer."

He grinned, he laughed, he looked relaxed and pleased with his comeback. McGrath and the announcers in the booth laughed even harder.

In a rematch of October's 30-20 thriller at Eugene, won by the unbeaten Hoosiers over the then second-ranked Ducks, a crowd of 75,604 almost exclusively wearing crimson-and-cream wildly cheered as Indiana turned three turnovers into touchdowns and built a 35-7 halftime lead in the College Football Playoff semifinal. The fans cheered, sang and laughed throughout a second half devoid of drama and filled with more domination.

"I thought it was just red seats," Oregon QB Dante Moore said, "but it was Indiana fans."

After the pick-six, Moore showed why his draft stock continued to rocket, leading a 14-play, 75-yard drive over 7½ minutes and throwing a 19-yard touchdown pass on a third-and-12.

With 7:11 left in the opening quarter, Mendoza finally touched the football. He needed three fewer plays and one minute less to cover the same distance, putting IU ahead 14-7 on an 8-yard pass to Omar Cooper Jr.

An exchange of punts gave the Ducks (11-3) the ball on their 13. Then the Ducks gave away their season.

On first down, Moore dropped back to throw, faked a handoff, hit the nose of the football on the back's left arm while trying to sling a pass. The ball dribbled to the 3, where Mario Landino pounced on it.

Three 1-yard runs by Kaelon Black made it 21-7.

Sacks near midfield by Dominique Ratcliff and Daniel Ndukwe ended the Ducks' next drive. Three plays, all completions by Mendoza, moved the ball to the Oregon 36. He was 7 of 8 for 66 yards ... and it was time to go deep. Charlie Becker dashed down the right sideline, climbed the ladder at the goal line, made the grab while falling backward and the lead was 28-7 with 4:57 left in the half.

Briefly. Two plays later, Ndukwe's strip sack of Moore put the ball on the turf again and Landino fell on it again

Just Ducky. Just Peachy. Coach Curt Cignetti and the Hoosiers collect more hardware for the trophy case in Bloomington with a 34-point victory over Oregon in the Peach Bowl. Up next: The CFP championship game against 10th-seeded Miami (Florida). GRACE HOLLARS/INDYSTAR

Chick-fil-A
PEACH
BOWL
CHAMPION

at the Oregon 21. On third-and-goal from the 2, Mendoza connected with Elijah Sarratt for a 35-7 edge with 59 seconds before the half.

Moore blamed himself for Friday night's unravelling: "First thing is first, the quarterback has to protect the ball. They have a great defense, great disguise and different looks, but you can't win football games if you're causing turnovers."

A year earlier, as the CFP's top seed and unbeaten, the Ducks trailed Ohio State by four touchdowns at the halftime in the Rose Bowl. They lost to the eventual champions 41-21.

"It's probably too premature for me to speak on what happened tonight," Oregon coach Dan Lanning said, "until I go back and really evaluate it."

Ndukwe turned out to be an unlikely but needed hero for the Hoosiers. A sophomore defensive end from Lithonia, Georgia, Ndukwe mainly played special teams behind edge-rushing stars Kellan Wyatt, whose season ended with a knee injury in the Michigan State game, and Stephen Daley, who suffered a serious leg injury jumping to high-five fans after the Big Ten title game.

"I got the XP boost in my body," Ndukwe said with laugh about playing near his hometown. "I knew we would have a great game. We delivered."

He finished with three tackles, two sacks and a force fumble. Plus, early in the final quarter, he blocked a punt that gave IU the ball at Oregon's 7. Three plays later, on a 3-yarder to Sarratt, Mendoza threw his fifth TD pass.

Ndukwe said he told teammate Byron Baldwin Jr. before the snap, "Let's go block it." Afterward, Ndukwe told reporters: "I think that shows a lot of character of who you are, what you do on special teams, not taking a play off even though we were up multiple scores."

The big night by a big man at 6-feet-3, 244 pounds didn't surprise defensive coordinator Bryant Haines. "He was a receiver in high school," Haines said. "You talk about hip fluidity, balance, spin, body control, all those traits that Cig talks about, he has those. Now we are just seeing them in real time."

Because of the Ducks' turnovers and two 75-yard drives while down at least five touchdowns, Oregon actually out-gained Indiana 378-362. But the Hoosiers (15-0) converted 11 of 14 third downs, scored touchdowns on seven of their 10 drives (not counting a game-ending kneel-down) and rushed for 231 yards (discounting an ugly sack-fumble-recovery that lost 20 yards).

With pinpoint accuracy (17 of 20 for 177 yards), the five TD tosses and a 21-yard run, Mendoza was an easy choice for the game's offensive most valuable player.

"That guy makes the right decisions," Lanning said. "He takes the ball where it's supposed to go, dictated by coverage. I think he did a great job again on scrambles early."

Despite Ndukwe's breakthrough game, the defensive MVP award went to Ponds, a junior cornerback from Miami (and James Madison). Besides his stunning pick-six, he made six tackles (four solo) and a half-tackle for loss. He also had a pick-six against Washington in 2024.

On IU's final drive before the half, Ponds lined up as a wide receiver on third-and-3 at the Oregon 14. He motioned into the backfield, turned to his right, caught a little swing pass at the 20 and made a first down at the 8.

"They're an unbelievably well-coached team," Lanning said. "You see a really complete team."

Cignetti raised his two-year record at Bloomington to 26-2. His demeanor led a reporter to ask before the Peach Bowl whether he ever was happy. He answered: "A lot of times, I'm happy. I just don't show it. I'm happy."

He seldom looked happy on the sideline with hands on hips and a scowl. He offered an explanation: "If I'm to ask my players to play the first play and play 150 the same regardless of the circumstances, then I can't be seen on the sideline high-fiving people and celebrating or what's going to happen? That's why I am the way I am.

"People ask, 'Do you ever get to enjoy this?' We just won and I've got 10 press conferences. When do I get to enjoy it? I do smile and I am happy at times."

He showed it Friday night. As his on-the-field interview wrapped up, ESPN's McGrath said: "Enjoy that beer, coach." Grinning from ear to ear, Cignetti said "thanks" and headed to pick up the Peach Bowl trophy. ■

— Gene Myers, Chris Hansen, Aaron Ferguson and Zach Osterman contributed.

Fernando Mendoza continued his torrid streak of lethal efficiency against Oregon, completing 17 of 20 passes for 177 yards and five touchdowns. Discounting a sack, he rushed five times for 48 yards. He was selected offensive MVP of the Peach Bowl. GRACE HOLLARS/INDYSTAR

CHAMPS

SURROUNDED BY GREATNESS: INDIANA'S REMARKABLE TWO-YEAR JOURNEY TO THE VERGE OF A NATIONAL CHAMPIONSHIP HAS UNIFIED FANS OF ALL SORTS

BY ZACH OSTERMAN

Greg Campbell, Indiana's sports information director for football, gestured emphatically, his eyes darting across the Mercedes-Benz Stadium seats.

Far from empty, they were crawling not just with joyous Indiana fans, but also celebrating Indiana players. In small packs, the Hoosiers had climbed the stairs leading up from the field to hug friends and family and generally just share this moment with anyone willing, because what is the point of any of this if it is done alone?

It can't be, really, and everyone knew that as they slapped hands and embraced and drank in this so thoroughly unbelievable moment — Indiana football, dominant and merciless, will play for a national championship Jan. 19 at Miami Gardens, Florida.

But Campbell needed to get his players into their locker room, so postgame media duties could be attended. After that, Chick-Fil-A and recovery drinks on the way to the bus, to a plane back to Bloomington, because there is one more job left.

The journey is not over. It is nonetheless remarkable.

"We ain't," Mark Cuban said on the field postgame, "done yet."

ALL SIGNS POINT TO A NATTY FOR CRIMSON AND CREAM

We are collectively, now, beyond any meaningful capacity for capturing the remarkability of this story.

It is one more victory from being perhaps the best American sports story ever witnessed, this tale so unbelievable as the team at its heart is unforgiving.

Top-ranked Indiana began Friday night's Peach Bowl, a College Football Playoff semifinal, by intercepting a Dante Moore pass on the game's first play and returning it for a touchdown. Nothing between that moment, when D'Angelo Ponds shrugged away Moore's token attempt at a tackle as his feet hit the end-zone turf, and the end of the game really mattered from there. The tone had been set, the terms made crystal clear:

Indiana was here on business, and Oregon was merely an allowed spectator. The final score of 56-22 reflected not even dominance but utter ruthlessness. Curt Cignetti's Hoosiers (15-0) dismissed Oregon with the minimum required effort, waving the Ducks away like a bug from a light.

"They're an unbelievably well-coached team," Oregon coach Dan Lanning said. "You see a really complete team, and I think they obviously have a chance to keep it going and have unbelievable success."

Fernando Mendoza was at his best, and if he is one more time, he's going to win a national championship in his hometown. He finished 17 of 20 for 177 yards and five touchdowns.

It was the sixth time this season Mendoza finished a game with as many or more touchdowns as incomplete passes. The Heisman complaints from some corners ring pretty hollow now.

"He was incredible," Cignetti said. "He was on top of the game."

Three sacks. Ten tackles for loss. Three forced turnovers, every one of them turned into a touchdown.

The mathematics of victory, laid down mercilessly and without prejudice. Again. Because that's just what this team is now. And, in all likelihood, what it will be one more time in 10 days.

But that's not what prompted the party in the stands.

Only recently thrust into a significant role because of injuries, defensive end Daniel Ndukwe filled the stat sheet with three tackles, two sacks, a forced fumble and a blocked punt. He was only a sophomore, although a big one at 6-feet-3 and 244 pounds. GRACE HOLLARS/INDYSTAR

ADIZERO

FROM COAST TO COAST, IU FANS TURN OUT IN DROVES

This is about more than points and yards. It has become something greater, to a fan base that longed for a moment like this.

We always envisioned that moment coming in a different kind of arena. It would not have been lost on at least some of the thousands and thousands — and thousands and thousands — of Indiana fans that painted Atlanta red this week that they once dreamed of winning a different kind of national championship here, only to lose to Maryland in the title game, in 2002.

Men's basketball has not been replaced in Bloomington, but it has been pushed aside. The center of the stage belongs to Cignetti's football program, rampant and arrogant and dominant.

It is giving this fan base something now it could only have ever dreamed of, wildly. And that fan base is meeting the moment by embracing all its dreams at once.

There is a communal quality to the whole thing. This isn't just about highlight reels and Heisman Trophies anymore. There is a journey, and these people — all these people — are on it together.

Filling the Rose Bowl with joyous song. Splitting tens of thousands of ears in Mercedes-Benz Stadium with their triumphant, conquering roar. Lining the streets of downtown Atlanta cheering their team's buses as they pass toward the stadium, and another casual on-the-field flattening.

Atlanta fancies itself the capital of college football. It probably is. And, on Friday, it found itself annexed by an alumni base that fancies itself the nation's largest, might be the nation's loudest and is certainly right now the sport's most ecstatic.

"Hoosier Nation is the best fan base in the entirety of college football," offensive tackle Carter Smith said in the locker room, with the cadence and gusto of a wrestling promoter. "They have traveled so well for us. They have been dying to see something like this. It's so great to be a part of something like this, that people are able to rally around and go across the nation.

"They went to California. They came down to Atlanta. They're going to be there next week in Miami. It's not going to be a home game for (the Hurricanes). I know that for sure. All that support is so amazing."

CUBAN SAYS HE GETS MORE THAN HE GIVES FROM IU

We love this sport because of what it conveys. It represents its places, its people and their cultures. What are you? You are a Bulldog. A Wolverine. A Trojan.

A Hoosier.

That means something fundamental and foundational, rooted at the very center of your soul.

There are thousands of people on this journey together right now. They come, as John Mellencamp intoned, from the cities and also the smaller towns. They flew to Los Angeles from New York and Boston and Japan, and they convoyed from Bloomington to Atlanta. They are sharing these moments and will hold them for the rest of their lives.

Because this is more than what they love. It is who they are.

Cuban, one of IU's most prominent and wealthy alums, gave a significant gift to Indiana recently, larger even than the one he delivered last year that made justifiable waves then. It paled, he said, in comparison to the gift given back.

"When you're around greatness, and you have a chance to participate with an organization that's special, it's just fun to be a part of," said Cuban, a star of "Shark Tank" and former owner of the Dallas Mavericks. "When it's a team I grew up with, basically, from the time I was 18 years old, to be a part of this, well, just wow. I'm glad people appreciate it, but what it gives me is far more than anything I could give to IU.

"No one would know who the hell I am if it weren't for Indiana University. Everything I've accomplished started at IU."

How many people in the stands Friday could say the same thing? How many feel that debt — and also that pride? Sports have the ability to become something more, to convey importance beyond simply what happens between their end zones and sidelines.

And this one — that comes to represent people and places, their values as well as their dreams — rises miles beyond the limits of a box score.

"It's the journey for IU," said Pam Whitten, the university's president. "We've got one more to win."

IU'S MARCH OF A LIFETIME UNIFYING FOR SO MANY

There is one more. Miami, in Miami Gardens, with eternity waiting on the other side.

Indiana spent years tagged as the losingest program

Star quarterback Fernando Mendoza and TV star Mark Cuban relish the glory of another CFP blowout. Cuban, besides his role on "Shark Tank," has a net worth in the billions. Mendoza, with an estimated $2.6 million in NIL deals, should cash in next as a high NFL draftee. GRACE HOLLARS/INDYSTAR

in college football history. The embodiment of perennial failure. That was Indiana football's identity.

But someone else took up that unfortunate burden this season, a reminder that so many of the things we are, are not permanent.

A championship is. That does not fade. Win and IU becomes the first 16-0 team in modern college football history. That is forever.

Scott Dolson, the athletic director who hired Cignetti from James Madison, often refers to the smoothy aligned values and support from the university's administration, to his department's, to Cignetti's program. Friday night — and the scene and emotion enveloping it from start to finish — was a reminder that there is another core constituency crucial to that success.

"Our fans," Dolson said, "are a huge part of this. The sacrifices they make to come out and support us, to pay for travel, to pay for tickets, to be here.

"It has been massive. I really can't adequately express what it means to us."

The moments shared postgame between those on the field and those in the stands — and those climbing up from the field into the stands — expressed what, with mere words, Dolson could not.

Indiana football is on the journey of a lifetime, marching toward forever, and no one is wasting a moment. ■

— Michael Niziolek contributed.

COLLEGE FOOTBALL PLAYOFF NATIONAL CHAMPIONSHIP
NO. 1 INDIANA 27, NO. 10 MIAMI (FLORIDA) 21
JANUARY 19, 2026 • MIAMI GARDENS, FLORIDA

SWEET 16!

HOW INDIANA'S CHAMPIONSHIP DREAMS BECAME REALITY IN A MOST FITTING FASHION

BY ZACH OSTERMAN

This is the dream.

This moment. This pregnant pocket of time, where everything is possible and so anything is possible.

The football you play as a child. The fantasy lived a thousand times alone. The glorious image in your head.

The game on the line, that game your responsibility, the only stakes being the largest ones imaginable.

In your backyard. In spring practice. In the summer heat and the winter cold, and now, on an unusually chilly Miami night, up six points with forever in sight.

This is the dream. Jamari Sharpe is about to grab it with both hands.

A GREAT AMERICAN SPORTS STORY

Indiana 27, Miami 21.

Fans will write it into their memories. Some will write it on their bodies in time.

There will be tall tales and where-where-yous, for a program whose entire history told us this would never happen.

The noise when Mikail Kamara blocked that punt, and Isaiah Jones fell onto it. The collective awe, as Fernando Mendoza bulldogged through the toughest defense he had played all season, shouldering a Hurricane to the turf on his way to what center Pat Coogan later described as "probably the greatest play in the history of Indiana football."

That moment the ball hit Sharpe's hands, then Sharpe the Hard Rock Stadium grass, melting away generations of frustration, misery and pain.

What does this mean? How to answer a question like that. Like trying to explain what it felt like when the mountain finally moved.

Across the course of the first 16-0 season in modern college football history, we've worked for some collective understanding of what's happened to college football's standard bearer for failure in a sport that only celebrates success. Whether anyone adequately has wrapped arms around that, contextualized it appropriately, is difficult to say.

The good news is we have a lifetime to try. Because this is one of the greatest stories American sports ever has told.

Ali in Zaire. Team USA in Lake Placid. The Indiana Hoosiers in Miami. We will talk about this team forever.

MISFITS FIT PERFECTLY ON A CHAMPION

Forever happened the hard way Monday night at Miami Gardens, Florida.

No. 10 Miami (Florida) made this the fight of everyone's life, that long, strong offensive line leaning and driving, and Rueben Bain Jr. just destroying everything in sight.

If he could get his hands on it, he wrecked it, and he had help. Miami (13-3) sacked Mendoza three times, pressured him so many more. He bled from his lip after a missed targeting call. He doubled over in pain more than once.

More than anyone else this season — more than Iowa, Oregon, Alabama or Ohio State — Miami made Indiana pay an absolute premium for victory.

The Hoosiers delivered every dollar and cent.

"The best D-line I've ever played, one of the most physical," Coogan said later. "All the credit to Miami. I mean, we knew it, but then it's like, holy (expletive).

"But that's football, baby. We came out on top."

Coogan was here a year ago, staring into the doubt-filled darkness Hurricanes grappled with Monday night.

Tight end Riley Nowakowski stands tall after his goal-line plunge gave Indiana a 10-0 second-quarter lead. It was only his second carry of the season. Against Kennesaw State, he also scored from the 1. GRACE HOLLARS/INDYSTAR

INDIANA
37

Notre Dame's starting center in the 2025 national championship game, Coogan spent those painful moments growing — whether he realized it or not — into a player and a man Indiana could not have done this without.

"You never really understand why. Why me? Why did we have to lose?" Coogan said. "It's hard to understand. It's a tough moment in time. It's a learning moment, but you don't learn from it until you're out of the moment. In the moment, it's just pain and misery."

And now?

"Just really grateful," he said, "for it all."

There are so many stories like that on this team. Under-recruited players. Transfers. The doubted and forgotten.

From their coach on down, the Hoosiers have been "misfits" (a word Coogan used before the victory at Purdue) fitted perfectly to this team, this moment and themselves.

Through the confetti and the hardware and the tears Monday night, they told that most remarkable, unforgettable story.

"It just shows you what technique, will — indomitable will — can do for a group," said defensive tackles coach Pat Kuntz. "Those guys battled their hearts out."

THE TITLE SPARKS MEMORIES OF FAMILY

Mark Deal cried tears of joy on the Lucas Oil Stadium field 45 days and what seems like a lifetime ago. The ones streaming from his eyes Monday carried something so much heavier.

As he celebrated in Indianapolis last month, Deal — one of the longest-tenured members of Indiana's athletic department and, specifically, its football support staff — delighted in the family ties then finally bound. His father, Russ, had captained the 1945 Big Ten champions. His brother, Mike, had played on the 1967 Big Ten champions. That night, Mark Deal finally won a Big Ten championship, too.

Now Mark Deal is the first Deal to win a national championship. And there was a heaviness that washed away as he explained, through those tears, what it meant.

"I think about my dad," Deal said. "I think about my son."

His son, Casey, is in Guatemala, doing missionary work and studying to be a priest. He has been there four years.

Mark texted Casey before the game with a prediction he shared elsewhere, too.

"I was gonna cry either way," he said. "If we lost, I was gonna cry, and I knew if we won, I'd cry."

Now he is, and he's not alone.

James Bomba fought back his own tears in those same rapturous moments as confetti blanketed the damp grass.

"Growing up, this was something you didn't even dream of," Bomba said, as the chorus to ABBA's "Fernando" rang through Hard Rock Stadium. "As an Indiana fan, there were a lot of hard times, a lot of hard days."

Like Deal, Bomba's legacy runs deep into the heart of Indiana's football history.

His father, Matt, played for Bill Mallory. Both of his grandfathers wore Indiana colors on scholarship. His father's father, Brad, also a member of the IU hall of fame, died last year.

"I know he's got a front seat up in heaven," Bomba said, joyous disbelief in his eyes. "It's just unbelievable."

These tears relieved something genuinely generational. Sports, like so much of our daily walks, are a thing we pass down. Something fundamental, something in the soul, between fathers and sons.

Their fathers walked the path before them, their brothers, their friends. Now Deal and Bomba were just two of an army of Hoosiers unburdening everyone of all of it.

Forever.

THE TOUGHEST TEAM IN COLLEGE FOOTBALL

Probably the greatest play in the history of Indiana football.

Maybe it was. Finding a Hoosier to argue against it would be an impossible task.

Mendoza's statue moment started where everything started for a Curt Cignetti team: scouting.

"Usually that was a third- or second-down call for us," offensive coordinator Mike Shanahan said of Mendoza's

Wide receiver Charlie Becker lets the Hurricanes know that he's a handful to cover. He gained 65 yards on four receptions, three of which were critical during Indiana scoring drives. GRACE HOLLARS/INDYSTAR

2026
NDIANA
80
24

draw. "It was something we saw earlier in the week, something in that third or fourth and high red (zone). We felt like it would have a chance to be a good play."

Indiana almost didn't run it at all. Cignetti called a time-out on fourth-and-4 to discuss his options.

Shanahan usually lobbies to go for it. IU's field-goal team was already on the field. Cignetti made up his mind and then made his mind known.

"Cignetti comes up," left tackle Carter Smith said, "and goes, 'We're going for it! Get off the field!'"

The call was a quarterback draw, with a tweak on blocking assignments to fit Miami's personnel. It's worked before, but never against a line this good.

And as with everything else Monday night, Miami made Mendoza earn it in his hometown. He finished the run planting Wesley Bissainthe into the turf.

"He showed his toughness again today," Shanahan said. "When the game's on the line, the ball's in his hands, you usually feel pretty good."

This was Mendoza's Heisman moment. Not the one that won him the award, but the one that validated that winning.

Tim Tebow. Cam Newton. Joe Burrow. He stands shoulder to shoulder with all of them now. Years into the future, when people ask what made Fernando Mendoza great, someone will show them that touchdown run, and they will understand.

And then they will watch this game, and through understanding Mendoza they will understand this team. So disciplined. So meticulous. So poised.

So tough.

Mikail Kamara bulldozing through for the first blocked punt-turned-touchdown in College Football Playoff history. Coogan wearing a towel damp with his blood. Mendoza, the superstar, the future No. 1 NFL draft pick, stretching his body past the point of safety in pursuit of perfection.

Indiana did not win because Indiana was the most talented team or because Indiana had the best plan. It might have been those things, but they were secondary.

At the final hurdle, Indiana was the best team, because Indiana was the toughest team. In the stadium and in the country.

Let that sit with you for the rest of your lives. It will follow them for the rest of theirs.

HAINES KNEW CIGNETTI COULD WIN AT IU

So, let's ask again, how was this possible? Maybe the better question, or at least the easier one to answer, is why.

"I felt like they were trying. I felt like they were starting to understand what was necessary to be successful," said defensive coordinator Bryant Haines, who spent time as a graduate assistant at IU and then later Ohio State. "Then you see the disparity between the two. You see Ohio State, they're like three gears ahead, and you go back to Indiana and they're still fighting for gear one.

"But I saw the want-to."

Years later, his boss would tell Haines he was considering leaving James Madison for Indiana.

In that moment, Haines gave Cignetti his honest opinion.

"What I told him," Haines said, "is you could win a lot of football games there."

Fred Glass believed this was possible. Kevin Wilson believed this was possible. Tom Allen believed this was possible.

None of them realized this moment, but they all envisioned it, and each of them in some way contributed to the journey from however we describe Indiana's pre-Cignetti existence to winning a national championship.

These Hoosiers have showed the world something once believed to be impossible never truly was. Can there really be any achievement greater than that?

OVERLOOKED MIAMI KID SEALED 'CANES FATE

The final drive, then.

Smith watched nervously, his false start penalty the primary reason Indiana hadn't salted the game away on its last possession.

In the fourth quarter on a fourth-and-4 from the Miami 12, Fernando Mendoza lunges for the end zone to score what will go down as the most memorable touchdown in the history of Indiana football. RICH JANZARUK/HERALD-TIMES

15
2026

They did not need to worry. Their defense wanted this moment, every bit of it.

"I told the guys, 'If we get one more shot,'" linebacker Aiden Fisher said, "'we're gonna go win it.'"

Haines let Fisher do most of the talking in the huddle, after Nico Radicic's field goal pushed the lead to 27-21.

But Haines delivered one clear, confident message.

"We're gonna play coverage," he told his defense. "We're gonna make (quarterback Carson Beck) try to earn it, and we're gonna rob him.

"We're gonna take his money at some point."

The call on the pick was a soft Cover 2, with safeties high.

Both of Indiana's starting corners are from Miami. Sharpe is the lesser known. He played at Northwestern, a football powerhouse in a powerhouse part of the country.

Like Smith and a handful of others, Sharpe came to Bloomington to play for Allen but stuck around. Only seven of the 23 original members of his signing class still wore cream and crimson Monday, and only six never left at all.

Haines watched as Sharpe — overlooked by his hometown program and now about to break its collective heart — played his technique perfectly. Jam, funnel, carry, just like corners coach Rod Ojong taught a thousand times in a hundred practices forgettable until they weren't.

Until this moment.

Beck lifted the ball in the air, taking a downfield shot he probably didn't need to. What he wouldn't have known, even as he watched his pass die toward the outstretched arms sprouting from a crimson jersey, is that Jamari Sharpe drops these a lot.

It turns out, Sharpe is one of IU's most consistent defensive backs in practice — he drops passes all the time.

"We always get on Sharpe because of how many passes he drops in practice," said safety Amare Ferrell, who watched the play from his spot in high zone. "And he catches it when we need it the most."

In 1979, Indiana had a defensive back named Tim Wilbur who teammates swore never won a foot race until he was in pads. Then he was uncatchable.

He was one of the best punt returners in IU history, no return more important than what turned out to be the game winner in the Holiday Bowl that season.

When teammates saw the back of Tim Wilbur's jersey that night in San Diego, they knew where he was going. And when teammates saw the ball floating into Sharpe's hands Monday night, they knew the same.

"Jamari doesn't have the best hands," Haines said, "but he has good hands when you need him to."

That Holiday Bowl was Indiana's first postseason victory. There had only been two more before this season, the last in 1991.

The program that started playing football in 1899 matched its entire postseason success before this season in a month.

And in the moment that mattered most, the one every child dreams of, the ball settled softly into Sharpe's waiting arms. As he lay down in grass, the world around him embraced forever with both arms.

One more overlooked Hoosier, proving the world was wrong to doubt him. A fitting ending. ■

Star cornerback D'Angelo Ponds takes in the championship scenery after beating Miami on its home field at Hard Rock Stadium to capture the national championship. RICH JANZARUK/HERALD-TIMES

2026
B1G
INDIANA
5